YOU, THE
INTRAPRENEUR

to my wife Elisa,

and our boys Eddie, Amedeo, Albie.

Thank you!

The cover features chamois climbing a mountain, serving as a metaphor for the intrapreneur's journey. Just as the chamois ascend steep cliffs with precision and balance, an intrapreneur steadily increases their value within the business, unlocking new career opportunities along the way. The chamois perfectly symbolize the ability to maintain balance and resilience, even on the most challenging and unstable paths.

Contents

Introduction 7

The Intrapreneurial Mindset 17

Communication and Relationship Building 25

Action, Problem-Solving and Innovation 43

Navigating Business Realities 53

Working in the Modern World 65

Personal Development and Professional Growth 83

Creating a Legacy and Making an Impact 97

The Intrapreneur 107

Handbook 109

Recommendations 117

Introduction

I am Andrea Magrini, a husband and a father of three, devoted to my family and building a successful future for them. Born in Italy and naturalized British, I have always been passionate about business and entrepreneurship. During my undergraduate studies in Italy, I made the decision to move to the UK to join the family business. However, this transition wasn't without its challenges. During my first year in the UK, I had to juggle between working and flying back to Italy to sit exams for my degree. It was during one of these trips in early 2000 that my life took an unexpected turn. I was involved in a car accident that left me with serious injuries and required multiple surgeries. The road to recovery was long and difficult, and it took about twelve months of physiotherapy for me to walk properly again. Despite the challenges, I was determined to get back on my feet when my Italian business commitments took over, and I never got the chance to sit for my final thesis submission. While I may not have technically graduated, the experience taught me valuable lessons and shaped me into the determined and resilient businessman I am today.

Growing up in a family owning a business forged me forever seeing what hard working looked like and the opportunities it offered: I was always going to join it! When I was a kid I remember answering the usual question of my parents' friends "what will you do when you grow up?" and I was going "I will be a shelving man!"...... yes, the family business was and still is shelving, for retail environments.

When I joined the Italian company in 2001, the business was moulded around my father style and it was agreed that it was a bit too small to survive and a bit too large for the lack of delegation. Ambition and lots of dedication and hard work, and the story unfolded:

2001-2005. Learn and implement what delegation is like, hiring colleagues for sales and technical design;

2006-2010. Expand on delegation and management structure, built a new large factory that would convince visiting clients we were a trustworthy supplier, survive the 2008 crash, prospect and onboard more export clients;

2011-2014. Launch a new investment round to automatically manufacture more products while realising that our satellite UK business was in deep financial trouble. If it was to fail, the Italian company would fail too, everything would be lost and nearly 100 people and friends would lose their job!

2014. While commuting to the UK every week to try and fix the situation, things weren't getting better that quickly. My wife was ok with my absences until she said "I guess we should all go?"

2015-2019. Moved with my wife and kids to the UK to successfully complete a company turnaround. My wife didn't speak English nor did my kids. She went to a school for immigrants to learn the language while the boys were thrown into school to figure it out themselves!

2020-2024. Transformed the UK company into a complete "retail display solution" business, with plenty of volume yet flexible manufacturing machineries to cater to UK retailers quickly, with standard and custom requirements.

As I reflected on my time at the company, I realized that my greatest accomplishment was not just the successful turnaround, but the transformation of the UK branch into a complete "retail display solution" business. It was a massive undertaking, but with my team's hard work and dedication, we were able to implement flexible manufacturing machinery and increase our volume to meet the demands of UK retailers. This expansion not only provided our clients with standard display solutions, but also customized options to fit their unique requirements. Moving to the UK with my wife and kids was a big decision, but it proved to be the perfect environment for this new chapter in my career. With a diverse and dynamic market, I was able to utilize my curiosity and love for learning to constantly improve and adapt our company's offerings. Working with colleagues, suppliers, and clients from different backgrounds and skillsets allowed for a rich exchange of ideas and perspectives, ultimately leading to our success. Managing a small business is a constant juggling act, but I thrive on the challenges and opportunities it presents. Every day brings something new, and I am constantly learning and growing as a leader. It is a role that requires a unique blend of skills and experiences, and I am grateful for the opportunity to have taken on such a rewarding and fulfilling position.

At the time of writing the UK business employs around 50 staff, everyone calls everybody else by name, we supply a mature product to a mature market and I class it as a small business.

Small and Medium Enterprises (SME) are the fabric of the economy, there are millions of small businesses and altogether they are the key player in the employment market. The following is from the Federation of Small Businesses:

"At the start of 2023 there were 5.6 million small businesses in the UK (with 0 to 49 employees), 99.2% of the total business population. SMEs account for 99.9% of the business population (5.6 million businesses).

SMEs account for three-fifths of the employment and around half of turnover in the UK private sector.

Total employment in SMEs was 16.7 million (61% of the total), whilst turnover was estimated at £2.4 trillion (53%).

Employment in small businesses (with 0 to 49 employees) was 13.1 million (48% of the total), with a turnover of £1.6 trillion (36%)."

The following chart explains the situation in a bit more detail: while large corporations take the stage for turnover and employment, micro small and medium companies remain crucial for the economy.

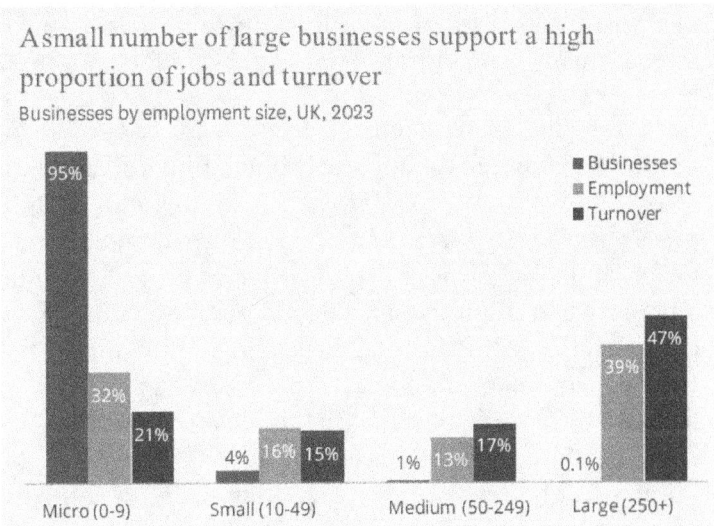

Source: DBT, Business population estimates, 2023. Turnover excludes the financial services sector.

The website money.co.uk (at the page www.money.co.uk/business/business-statistics) gives an insight of the actual ownership of SMEs: "a recent UK business report found that, in 2021, 80% of SMEs were defined as family-owned businesses – up from 77% in 2020. Of the smaller enterprises, 82% of micro-businesses were considered family-owned, along with 69% of small businesses and 57% of medium-sized companies".

If you work in the private sector there is a 60% chance that you work in a micro, small or medium-sized company and an 80% probability that the business is family owned. It's therefore very likely that the environment you work in is very similar to the one of my company. The managing director owns all or most of the company shares and is directly involved in the day to day dynamics of the business.

Over the years, I have been able to create many meaningful business systems. I have learned how to build delegation systems, export sales all over the world, and nurture management structures. My work life experience is very varied and I'm privileged to what life has thrown at me! This has allowed me to gain a deeper understanding of the dynamics of a company and how to effectively manage it. In my years of experience, I have also learned how to navigate through challenging financial situations. This has been vital in ensuring the growth and success of the businesses I have worked for. My skills extend beyond just management, as I have also been involved in the creation of sales agency structures and the building of a factory from scratch. These experiences have equipped me with the ability to understand workflows and implement ERP systems and product configurations. Overall, my diverse experience in different areas of business has given me a well-rounded understanding of the intricacies of a company. This has allowed me to effectively contribute to the success of the businesses I have worked for. With my expertise and knowledge, and the amazing team around me, I am confident that further business and colleagues' growth lies ahead.

Every person has a unique life story and different experiences that shape their knowledge, but I believe the people you work with and for are very similar to me. They share the joys and challenges of owning and managing a business—and the hurdles that come with it.

The hope is that those working closely with me enjoy doing so: over the years we have 'learned from each other' and improved how to portray ourselves, our frustrations, our ideas, I suppose this is how loyalty to a business is built. During one of my self-challenging sessions, while driving the car or reading a book, I ended up asking myself: "<u>have I ever told my colleagues how I expect them to be, with me, with the business?</u>".

Each company has a different onboarding process, there can be company manuals, often focusing more on the HR side of things, there are training documents, then KPI etc etc. But what about all of the other soft elements of one's life at work?

If you are a business owner or company director, have you managed to express your view of things, what you look for in a successful colleague?

If you work for a business owner, since you're certainly somewhere in an organization chart reporting line, have you been told the soft elements of your character, your behaviour that the business would desire, both of which will nurture company growth and subsequently, your personal professional growth?

Most often, the answer to the above questions is no. As an employee, it can be easy to get lost in the daily tasks and forget about the bigger picture. However, as a successful colleague, it is important to take a step back and consider the soft elements of your character and behaviour that your business and employer would desire. This includes things like leadership, adaptability, and problem-solving skills. By focusing on these qualities, you can help nurture company growth and in turn, your own personal and professional growth. It is for this reason that I thought of writing this book. It contains elements I learned from books, training courses, and exchanges with people around the world. I have also included the mistakes I've made along the way, in the hopes of providing a more complete picture. My goal is to share with you how a business owner and director thinks, and most likely expects from you as an employee. By understanding their perspective and focusing on the soft skills they desire, you can become a successful colleague and contribute to the growth of your company.

As a business owner or director, I strive to create a successful and thriving company. As an employee, understanding my perspective and the soft skills that I desire can help you become a valuable member of our team. You have the potential to contribute to the growth of the company and become a successful colleague. My book focuses on providing you with insights on how I think and what I expect from my colleagues, so you can achieve your own personal growth and success within the company. Having said that, there are countless self-growth books available that promise to help you achieve success. However, my book is different in the sense that it is specifically tailored towards employees working in a family-owned and run SME. The examples and advice I provide are relatable to your everyday life and experiences, rather than the corporate world that is often depicted in other self-help books. I understand the challenges and dynamics of working in a smaller business, and my book aims to provide you with practical and applicable tips for success. My intention is not to be a star writer or achieve any sort of fame through this book. Instead, my goal is to share my knowledge and insights with you, in the hopes of helping you reach your full potential within the company. So, keep your curiosity high and continue reading for your personal growth and success as an employee.

I am Andrea Magrini and yes, I've achieved some business success. I go to work every day at 8.30. When I'm on holiday I am mostly reachable and try to stay on top of emails and messages daily. I don't play golf and I'm not part of the country club. I fly low cost and economy in long haul flights. I drive a nice car and I keep it for six or seven years to lower the overall cost of ownership. My kids go to public schools. I love sailing but I can't afford the luxury of a yacht sat in a marina waiting for me to sail it a few days a year.

The overarching thought about this book is to give you an insight of how your average business owner thinks about and expects off colleagues, to close that gap between the entrepreneur and their employees, leveraging on their characters to trigger intrapreneurial behaviours. This is written by your average business owner and director, who's done relatively well for himself but remains within reach.

Chapter 1

The Intrapreneurial Mindset

"The best way to predict the future is to create it."

Abraham Lincoln

The importance of SMEs in the country's economy cannot be overstated. They make up a significant portion of the GDP and provide employment for a large number of individuals. These companies, typically owned and managed by a single person or a family, can have a long-standing presence in the market or be newly established. As they continue to grow, the owner often finds themselves in need of additional help to manage day-to-day tasks. As the owner starts to delegate tasks to their employees, a potential issue arises: the gap between their expectations and the employee's understanding on deliverables. This can happen especially in cases where the tasks are repetitive and may seem mundane to the employee. It is crucial for the employer to effectively communicate their expectations and provide clear instructions to avoid any misunderstandings. To bridge this gap and ensure smooth operations, it is important for the employer to establish a good working relationship with their employees. This includes providing proper training and guidance, setting clear goals and expectations, and fostering open communication. By doing so, the employer can ensure that their employees have a thorough understanding of their role and responsibilities within the company. In turn, this can lead to increased productivity, job satisfaction, and a stronger sense of loyalty towards the company. SMEs play a vital role in the economy, and it is essential for employers to nurture a positive and productive work environment to sustain their growth.

In today's competitive business world, it is crucial for companies to have a team of dedicated and motivated individuals who are willing to go the extra mile to achieve success. As an employee, taking on responsibilities within the company not only helps to contribute to the overall success of the business, but it also allows for personal growth and development. By being actively involved in various tasks and projects, employees are able to expand their skillset and gain valuable experience, making them an invaluable asset to the company. Furthermore, when employees take on additional responsibilities, it can lead to increased productivity and job satisfaction. When individuals are given the opportunity to take on new challenges and showcase their abilities, they are more likely to be engaged and motivated in their work. This positive attitude can have a ripple effect on the entire team, creating a more dynamic and efficient work environment. Additionally, when employees feel valued and trusted by their employers, it can foster a stronger sense of loyalty towards the company, leading to lower turnover rates and a more stable workforce. In the broader scope of the economy, small and medium-sized enterprises (SMEs) play a vital role in driving growth and creating job opportunities. As such, it is crucial for employers to nurture a positive and productive work environment to sustain the growth of their business. By investing in their employees and providing them with opportunities to take on responsibilities, SMEs can not only contribute to the success of their own company, but also to the overall growth and development of the economy.

Entrepreneurs are known for their entrepreneurial skills and creativity. In contrast, intrapreneurs are employees within a company who exhibit similar qualities, but operate under the umbrella of the organization. Intrapreneurship allows these individuals to take on more responsibilities and have a greater impact on the company's success. The concept of intrapreneurship is gaining popularity as companies strive to create a positive and productive work environment. Investing in employees and providing them with opportunities to think and act like entrepreneurs not only benefits the company, but also contributes to the overall growth and development of the economy. Intrapreneurship encourages employees to think outside the box and come up with innovative ideas and solutions. This, in turn, can lead to the development of new products or services, which can help the company expand and increase its market share. Intrapreneurship also fosters a culture of collaboration and teamwork within the company. Employees are encouraged to share their ideas and work together to bring them to life. This not only boosts morale and motivation, but also creates a sense of ownership and pride in the work being done. As a result, employees tend to be more engaged and committed to the company's success, leading to a more positive and productive work environment. Intrapreneurship, therefore, plays a crucial role in sustaining the growth of businesses and contributing to the overall economy.

During a graduation speech Steve Jobs invited students to 'connect the dots'; it's a very good speech and I invite you to watch it online. During my work I keep engaging with that line of thinking, whether it's about connecting people I know with different skillsets that would complement each other, or how sales purchase and cash flows connect with one another.

In my work, I have found that the key to success is to always consider the long-term implications of every decision I make. It's important to not just focus on what will benefit the business today, but also what will set it up for even greater success in the future. This is a mindset that I consistently apply in my daily responsibilities, whether it's connecting people with complementary skillsets or analyzing how various aspects of the business, such as sales and cash flows, are interconnected. I have seen this approach pay off in many instances, especially in family businesses where the goal is to ensure the longevity and prosperity of the company for future generations. It's important to think beyond just the next few quarters and years and instead consider the impact of our actions a decade or even two decades down the line. By breaking down this concept into smaller, daily tasks, I am able to ensure that I am not just focused on short-term gains, but also building a strong foundation for the business to thrive in the long run. Ultimately, it is the intrapreneur responsibility to not just focus on the present, but also have a strategic and forward-thinking mindset. This means completing tasks and making decisions that will benefit the business now, without sacrificing its potential for growth and success in the future. By constantly thinking ahead and considering the long-term implications, I am able to contribute to the overall success and sustainability of the business in a meaningful way.

Sustainability is too often an misunderstood word, limited to topics around the environment. The UN definition of sustainability is "the ability to meet the needs of the present without compromising the ability of future generations to meet their own needs". This core concept applies to business across its every day operations and colleagues. A personal success that comes at the expense of a colleague's learning or performance will result in lower long-term value and is not sustainable. A new order that brings immediate results at the detriment of other smaller jobs from repetitive and long standing customers may also be non sustainable. Balancing short term and long term is a difficult challenge, since long term is only the result of many short terms. However, sustainability is crucial... on business operations, on relationships between colleagues. Success, including personal success, involves creating a thriving environment for everyone, not just the individual.

The sustainable approach is a mindset that should be applied to all aspects of life. When it comes to business operations, it is important to not only focus on short term success, but also consider the long term impact. This can be a difficult challenge, as the long term is only the result of many short terms. However, by constantly evaluating sustainability, we can create a thriving environment for everyone, not just ourselves. Sustainability is not just about the environment, it also applies to relationships between colleagues. In order for a company to be truly successful, it must foster a positive and sustainable work culture. This involves creating a sense of balance between personal success and the success of the team. By prioritizing sustainability, we can ensure that all individuals within the company are thriving and contributing to the overall success. In the pursuit of excellence and growth, it is important to continuously evaluate the sustainability of our actions. Before implementing any new processes, procedures, or products, we should always ask ourselves if it is sustainable. By doing so, we can ensure that we are creating a long-lasting and successful business that benefits not only ourselves, but also those around us.

When I developed my experience in the UK business environment I came across a short, incredible business lesson, told to me as "KISS = keep it stupid simple".

After a short research I found out this came from an extremely complicated environment of spy planes design.

Kelly Johnson is thought to have coined the phrase "Keep it simple, stupid" **(KISS)** in the 1960s. Johnson was the lead engineer at Lockheed Skunk Works, the aircraft manufacturer that created the Lockheed U-2 and SR-71 Blackbird spy planes. Johnson told his design team that the warplanes they were designing should be simple enough to be repaired by a mechanic in the field with basic tools and training. The "stupid" part of the phrase refers to the relationship between how things break and how sophisticated the repairs are.

The KISS principle is a design principle that states that simplicity is a key goal in design and unnecessary complexity should be avoided.

I believe that the intrapreneur should recommend tasks, operations and growth ideas with the KISS principle at heart. Simple things work better. They are understood better by current and future colleagues. The KISS principle can also be applied to the sales and marketing strategies of a company. In fact, Marketing Made Simple (look it up on the internet) has an interesting approach that revolves around keeping the message simple, clean and to the point. This is a great reinforcement of the idea that simple things just work better. When marketing and selling products or services, it is important to avoid unnecessary complexity and focus on a clear and concise message that can be easily understood by potential customers. This principle not only applies to the external communication of a company, but also to its internal operations and growth strategies. By keeping things simple, employees are more likely to understand and implement tasks and ideas suggested by their colleagues. This can lead to a more efficient and productive work environment. In addition, future colleagues who join the company will have an easier time adapting and understanding the existing processes and strategies if they are kept simple and straightforward. Therefore, the KISS principle can be seen as a key design principle that can benefit a company in various aspects.

Chapter 2

Communication and Relationship Building

The intrapreneur spends a significant amount of time at their job, striving to provide exceptional service to customers, whether through direct or indirect means. It is common to acknowledge that we are employed by or work on behalf of a company, but for the intrapreneur, it is more than just a job. It is a passion, a calling, a mission and a way of life. The drive to deliver excellence to clients is a defining characteristic of the intrapreneur. This pursuit often requires long hours, sleepless nights, and personal sacrifices. However, for the intrapreneur, it is all worth it to see the satisfaction on a client's face or to receive positive feedback for a job well done. The dedication and determination of the intrapreneur are what sets them apart from the average worker. While the intrapreneur may spend a large part of their life at work, it is not just about a pay check or climbing the corporate ladder. It is about making a difference, leaving a mark, and creating a legacy. The intrapreneur understands that their work has an impact not only on the company but also on the clients and the community. They take pride in their role and the responsibility that comes with it, constantly striving to exceed expectations and deliver excellence in all that they do.

The etymology of a word often sparks reflection, reminding us that we are not the first to give meaning to what we say. As an intrapreneur, reflecting on the legacy of those who came before us is critical. It's this understanding that helps us to recognize that our work has an impact not only on the company but also on the clients and the community. We take pride in our role and the responsibility that comes with it, constantly striving to exceed expectations and deliver excellence in all that we do. We understand that our actions today will shape the future for generations to come. As intrapreneurs, we are not just employees, but we are also innovators, change-makers, and leaders. We are constantly finding ways to improve processes, products, and services, always looking for ways to make a positive impact. We know that our work is not just about making a profit, but it's also about creating value for our customers and positively contributing to the community. Our legacy is not only about what we leave behind, but also about the relationships we build and the impact we make on the people around us. As an intrapreneur, we strive to leave a positive legacy that will inspire others to continue the tradition of excellence and innovation in our company. The word "company" comes from the Old French word "compagnie", which was first recorded in 1150. Compagnie comes from the Late Latin word "companion", which means "one who eats bread with you". Companio is a calque of the Germanic expression "gahlaibo", which literally means "with bread". The word "company" originally described how merchants would gather, share stories, eat together, and trade.

It's interesting how a simple word like "company" has such humble beginnings. Initially, the word "company" was used to describe merchants who would gather and share stories, eat together, and trade. It was a way for them to form a bond and trust with one another. This concept of coming together and forming a team has been ingrained in the idea of a company since its origin. Even today, the success of a company is highly dependent on the strength of its team and how well they work together. In the business environment, the word "company" has evolved to mean a body corporate, like a "limited company". However, at its core, a company is still a group of people who come together to achieve a common goal. The word "team" may have taken over, but the essence of what a company truly is remains the same. It is a gathering of individuals who share a common purpose and work together towards a shared vision.

The foundation of a successful company lies in the strength and collaboration of its team members. Each individual brings their own unique skills and perspectives to the table, but it is their shared goal and vision that binds them together. While the term "team" may be commonly used in the business world, its true essence remains unchanged - it is a group of people who come together to achieve a common purpose. In order for a company to thrive, effective communication among team members is crucial. This involves actively listening and engaging in open and honest dialogue, as well as utilizing the skills we have developed throughout our lives. From learning to speak and read as children, to honing our communication skills as we grow, these abilities are essential for the intrapreneur to navigate the complexities of the business world and effectively interact with stakeholders such as customers and suppliers. By leveraging the collective power of the company and continuously improving upon communication skills, the intrapreneur can drive sustainable success for both themselves and the organization as a whole. This fosters a sense of unity and shared purpose, creating a strong foundation for the company to achieve its goals and reach its full potential.

The primary methods of communication within a business are spoken and written. Spoken communication typically occurs in person or through video calls, while written communication can take place via email or other messaging platforms. The type of communication and the medium used greatly influence how we should convey our message. It is also important to consider whether the communication is one-on-one or one-to-many, and in the former, to whom we are communicating. Before communicating, it is essential to take a moment to reflect: am I addressing one individual or a group? If it is a group, who specifically? Am I composing an email, or is it better to use an internal post (one to many) or a one-on-one chat? In the latter, face to face or video? Choose the right medium!

First and foremost, the most crucial aspect of effective communication is the underlying reason behind it. What is the purpose of initiating or responding to a conversation? This "why" must be carefully considered. Often, when it comes to communication within a company, this aspect is overlooked. Is the intention to seek advice and share doubts, or is it simply to provide information? Is there a disagreement that needs to be addressed, or is it a different perspective on a specific topic? Are we seeking a quick answer or a more detailed response when asking for information? When it comes to communication not initiated by ourselves, one may think that responding to a question is just a formality and part of the job. However, there is more to it than that. Is the question actually requesting a more extensive explanation beyond a simple answer?

The intrapreneur works on their communications' skills. Firstly by choosing the appropriate medium. Then, whether it's verbal or written, one to one or one to many, digital or in person... the message has to be clear, to the point, in a way that help one achieve what's needed.

The art of being an intrapreneur requires a certain set of skills. One of the key skills is having strong communication skills. This involves being able to convey your message effectively, whether it be verbally or in written form. It is crucial to be able to communicate clearly and concisely in order to achieve your desired outcome. In order to be an intrapreneur, one must recognize the importance of clarity when communicating. Given the challenging environment of the workplace, it is important to be mindful of people's time and avoid any confusion. Additionally, when approaching someone for a specific reason, it is important to get straight to the point and not beat around the bush. This not only shows respect for the other person's time, but also helps in achieving one's desired outcome. When communicating as an intrapreneur, it is important to use plain language and avoid any complex jargon. This helps to ensure that your message is easily understood by everyone, regardless of their background or expertise. Additionally, making sure that sentences flow without any interruptions or interjections can make the message more impactful. As an intrapreneur, being able to effectively communicate with others is crucial in order to achieve success in any given situation. Verbal communication is a powerful tool that allows your personality to shine through while delivering a message. It is also more effective when complemented with body language. On the other hand, written communication should be tailored to the recipient's background and avoid using complex vocabulary. When sending emails with elaborate messages, it is recommended to structure the content by starting with the topic or main idea in one clear line, followed by additional information or questions. This way, the recipient can quickly grasp the purpose of the message and provide a more efficient response. To ensure clarity, it is important to keep the communication direct and concise. Effective communication is crucial for intrapreneurs to thrive in any given situation. This requires being able to convey ideas and information in a way that is easily understood by others, regardless of their background or expertise. Additionally, maintaining a continuous flow in the delivery of the message without interruptions or interjections can make it more impactful; this is relevant in both verbal (avoiding the "uh", "er"...) and written communications (avoiding to write as one would speak). This skill is especially important when working in a team or collaborating with others, as effective communication can foster understanding and drive success. Intrapreneurs must also be able to adjust their communication style according to the situation and the recipient, whether it is verbal or written, in order to achieve the desired outcome.

It happens quite often that I stare at an email or a message asking myself: "what are you telling / asking me?". When you write something, think of the other end, will they get it straight away?

This highlights the importance of considering the other end when formulating written communication. By doing so, it ensures that the message is clear, concise, and easily understood by the recipient, avoiding any potential misunderstandings. In today's digital age, communication has become more diverse, with various channels such as emails, instant messaging, and video conferencing being utilized. However, while these channels provide convenience and efficiency, they also come with their own set of challenges. For instance, written messages may not convey the intended tone, making it crucial to choose the right words and sentence structure to avoid misinterpretation. Additionally, the lack of immediate feedback in written communication can also lead to delays in decision-making and problem-solving. Therefore, it is essential to understand the differences between verbal and written communication and adapt accordingly to ensure effective communication in the workplace.

Has a meeting been organized? The organiser will turn up and prepare the room a good 10 minutes early and should start it by stating who is present and who isn't, how long will the meeting take but also what's the goal of the meeting. Whilst attendees and time are mentioned more often, the goal is often missed. Without a clear goal it's impossible to be certain if the meeting was successful or a waste of time. Meeting goals can vary: inform, discuss, decide, introduce a topic for colleagues to think and decide at a new meeting a week later. It's important that attendees arrive minimum 5 minutes early and then participate but the respect of the time allocated to the meeting remains crucial. A meeting is costly for everyone's time sake, it must flow with energy and participation. As the time nears the end, the goal has to be stated. Sometimes a meeting drags on with debate and challenges, without progressing. The meeting chair should call it off and re arrange after everyone will have reflected on it.

Something similar happens more often on emails: someone starts a thread with five or six colleagues, each one invests their time in reading and replying. Six, times six, time six, every consideration added to a reply multiplies the thread length. What was missing? The goal of the first email! It goes on and on, to waste valuable time. Call it off immediately, organise a meeting. My general rule is that any topic, discussion, decision is held verbally, preferably face to face otherwise videocall. The decision is then circulated on email; it's good practice to write such outcome (decision, information, debate) on the screen at the end of the meeting together, so the attendees know how is the email coming worded and that it's correct and that it won't spark yet another discussion.

And what about the quality of your email? I get so often forwarded emails where the subject doesn't make sense (i.e. FWD: Attachment), there is no comment from my sender and there's loads of text below, maybe few attachments. Basically, whoever sent that email to me, pretends that I read everything, find out the issue, formulate a decision. It's a big no-no for me. If you find yourself sending emails like this, think of the safety of your job! What did you add to it? How did you you're your colleagues work easier if you just pass things on? Please when sending an email think carefully and remain professional, constructive and save peoples time:

Carefully choose who goes in To and Cc

Subject: three of four words which don't just bring up the topic, but the reason for sending the email and the desired action from the meeting

Copy:

First line, one line: what are you asking? Informing? Or requesting a reply?

Give more context, in bullets, each one shorter than a line. Check your copy, is it crisp, clear, unequivocable, to the point?

Example.

Don't send email like this:

Subject: FWD: Detail analysis document

Copy 1: empty, just the message you received

Copy 2: many paragraphs with lots of words explaining stuff, and a spreadsheet attachment of 200kb with many columns and hundreds of lines

Send like this:

Subject: Supplier A - Accept 10% higher prices? - FWD: Detail Analysis document

Copy: Supplier A is asking for a 10% price increase. On an yearly basis this means spending xxx£ more.

Shall we accept?

I suggest we accept it.

Their data and explanations below make sense given the current market conditions. I compared the prices with two alternative suppliers, and other suppliers will deliver the same year spend or more.

Attached are:

Cost comparison between suppliers

Supplier A dataset.

* * * * * *

The example is obviously an invented scenario, but it shows how communications must remain constructive, with a clear purpose for it. What it is that you are asking? In the example, the buyer needs a decision to approve a price increase from a supplier. What do you suggest we do? In the example, the buyer suggests to accept it, because of valid reasons.

The purpose of this is to ensure that we are not communicating just for the sake of it. It is important to remember to be thoughtful about our words and how they will be perceived by the recipient. Instead of simply talking because we are asked to, we should always strive to be constructive and make sure our message is easily understood. This requires us to think about the context and how the other end will react to our words. In order to achieve effective communication, it is crucial to provide more context in our emails. This can be done by using bullet points, each one shorter than a line, to clearly outline our message. Additionally, we should always check our copy to make sure it is crisp, clear, and to the point. This will prevent any ambiguity or confusion in our communication. Whether we are asking a question, providing information, or requesting a reply, our words must be unequivocal in order to avoid any misunderstandings. As individuals in any industry, it is imperative that we always take the time to review our written communication before sending it out. This ensures that our message is conveyed without any ambiguity or confusion. In negotiations, it is especially important to stay ahead of the counterpart by anticipating their responses and addressing any potential concerns. This can also be applied to internal communications within a company. It is essential that we communicate with honesty, clarity, and respect, without resorting to coercion or manipulation. By keeping our communication clear and open, we can avoid any unnecessary conflicts and foster a positive and productive working environment. However, if a disagreement does arise, it is important to address it in a constructive manner. This means expressing our opinions and concerns while also considering the perspectives of others. By doing so, we can promote healthy discussions and reach a resolution that benefits all parties involved. Ultimately, clear and effective communication is crucial in any setting, whether it be in negotiations or within a company, to ensure that our messages are conveyed accurately and without any misunderstandings.

Effective communication is a fundamental aspect of any human interaction. It allows us to express our thoughts, feelings, and ideas effectively, and to understand and connect with others. In order to achieve this, it is essential to engage in healthy discussions where all parties involved have the opportunity to express their perspectives and opinions. This promotes a mutual understanding and paves the way for reaching a resolution that benefits everyone. In situations where there may be conflicts or differing opinions, it is important to ensure that our messages are conveyed accurately and without any misunderstandings. This is especially crucial in negotiations, where clear and effective communication can make all the difference in reaching a successful outcome. Within a company, effective communication is also vital for the smooth functioning of daily operations and for maintaining a positive and productive work environment. One way to ensure effective communication is by actively listening to the other person and seeking clarification when needed. This can be achieved by asking the recipient to repeat the content or by summarizing the key points of the discussion. Not only does this ensure that the message has been transferred correctly, but it also helps the recipient to remember and understand it better. By following these simple yet powerful techniques, we can enhance our communication skills and build stronger relationships with others.

Have you ever thought about the power of questions? Questions are powerful tools that can help us effectively communicate our thoughts and ideas. Closed questions, which suggest direct, dry answers, can be useful in certain situations. These questions help us get specific and precise information, but they can also hinder the flow of communication. On the other hand, open questions, which start with 'wh' words, encourage the other person to share their perspective and provide more detailed responses. This not only helps to facilitate better understanding between individuals, but also creates a more engaging and meaningful conversation. Asking open questions is a simple yet effective technique to enhance our communication skills and build stronger relationships with others. By asking open-ended questions, we show genuine interest in the other person's thoughts and feelings, and allow them to express themselves freely. This not only helps to establish a deeper connection, but also allows us to gain a better understanding of their perspective. As a result, we can build trust and foster stronger relationships with those around us. In conclusion, the power of questions cannot be underestimated. By using the right type of questions in our communication, we can not only ensure that our message is conveyed accurately, but also create a more meaningful and engaging conversation. So the next time you engage in a conversation, remember to use open questions to encourage the other person to express themselves and strengthen your relationship with them. This is pretty basic stuff and there's much more to it. Being able to formulate the right question delivers a huge amount of capacity, knowledge, rapport. Asking "what do you think of the match yesterday?" or "how do you think the teams performed yesterday?" sound the same but aren't. The first is open and vague, the second is more about the performance. Depending on who we are asking and what we want to achieve from the answer, the question needs calibrating very carefully. This can be done by exercising at home, writing questions about something but that come from different angles. When in a business discussion with colleagues clients suppliers or any stakeholder, we should train ourselves to always be ahead of the conversation and prepare the following questions carefully.

Practising at home and writing questions from different angles is a great way to calibrate your questions carefully.

By doing this, you can train yourself to always be ahead of the conversation when discussing business. This can lead to honest and constructive communications with your colleagues, which will elevate your character. When you are well-prepared with thought-provoking questions, it shows that you value the discussion and are genuinely interested in the topic at hand. Additionally, this approach can help you transition smoothly into various topics and conflicts that may arise during the conversation. By having different angles and points of view, you can prevent the discussion from becoming stagnant and repetitive. This will also allow you to expand on various plot points and give a more complete picture, providing meaningful contributions to the story. However, it is important to know when to quit. Once you have accomplished extending your points of view, major conflicts, and various plot points of the story, that is the time to end it. Continuously adding unnecessary details can disrupt the flow of the conversation and cause it to lose its purpose. Therefore, always keep in mind the purpose of your expansion and make sure it adds value to the overall discussion.

When engaging in a conversation, it's important to keep in mind the purpose of the discussion. Whether it's to share knowledge, provide advice, or find a solution to a problem, the goal should always be to leave the other person better off than before. This can be achieved by providing useful information, offering guidance, or even just giving a bit of hope during tough times. By doing so, we can make a positive impact on someone's life and help them grow in some way, however, it's also important to know when to stop. This can also make the other person feel overwhelmed or disinterested. Therefore, it's crucial to stay on track and only expand on points that are relevant and meaningful to the discussion. This way, we can ensure that the conversation remains engaging and purposeful. In conclusion, while it's important to expand on points during a conversation, it's equally important to do so with a purpose and in moderation. By being mindful of the other person's time and staying on track, we can have a meaningful and impactful conversation that benefits both parties involved. And remember, once you've accomplished extending points and resolving conflicts, it's time to end the conversation and let the other person walk away better off than before.

One valuable lesson I was once given was to ensure that every conversation I have with someone <u>leaves them in a better state than before</u>. This principle should be upheld in all discussions, regardless of the subject matter.. We all have conversations that leave us feeling worse than before. This simple principle can make a huge difference in someone's life. Imagine if every conversation you had left the other person with a bit of extra knowledge, advice, a problem sorted or nearing solution. This would not only make their day better, but it could also have a positive ripple effect on others. It's easy to get caught up in the subject matter of a conversation and forget about the impact it may have on the other person. However, we should always strive to make our conversations meaningful and beneficial for both parties. This could mean offering a different perspective, sharing a personal experience, or simply being a good listener. We never know what others may be going through in their life, and by focusing on making them better off, we can create a more positive and supportive atmosphere for everyone. Ultimately, this principle teaches us to be mindful of our words and actions, and the impact they can have on others. By striving to leave people better off than before, we can make a positive difference in someone's life, no matter how small. So the next time you have a conversation, remember this valuable lesson and make it a goal to walk away knowing that the other person has gained something from it. In order to leave people better off than before, we must make a conscious effort to have meaningful and positive conversations. This is not always easy, especially when the topic is controversial or adversarial. However, it is in these situations that our words can have the most impact. By approaching these conversations with empathy and understanding, we can make a positive difference in someone's life. Even in seemingly small and mundane conversations, we have the power to make a positive impact. Whether it's a simple conversation with a stranger or a deep discussion with a loved one, we can strive to walk away knowing that the other person has gained something from our exchange. This could be a new perspective, a deeper understanding, or simply feeling heard and valued. It is our responsibility to use our words wisely and leave others better off than before. Remembering this valuable lesson can bring purpose and intention to our conversations. By setting a goal to make a positive difference in someone's life, we can create meaningful connections and contribute to a more positive and understanding society. So the next time you have a conversation, no matter how big or small, try to make it a goal to leave the other person better off than before. Your words have the power to make a difference. When we strive to leave people better off after a conversation, we are not only contributing to their growth but also to the betterment of society as a whole. By making meaningful connections, we are fostering a more positive and understanding environment where people can truly thrive. So, whether it's a casual chat or a serious discussion, let's make it our goal to have a positive impact on others through our words. Each conversation we have is an opportunity to make a difference. By choosing our words carefully and with intention, we can uplift and empower those around us. This is especially important in the currently often disjointed world. By taking the time to truly listen and respond in a meaningful way, we can build stronger relationships and create a ripple effect of positivity in our communities.

Exercise.

Write a story about something, for example when you last walked the dog or how you spent your last holiday.

First write it with 50 words.

Put it aside, then write it in 30 words.

Then again, 15 words.

Then 10.

Then 5.

Do this a few times and notice, from 50 to 10 words that the core topic that you wanted to transfer over is still there!

Exercise example.

50 words

My wife and I spent the last weekend in London, visiting the British Museum, strolling around the city centre, enjoying a lovely lunch at an Italian restaurant, and buying gifts for our boys at Hamleys, our favourite London shop, making the most of a perfect day together in the heart of the city.

30 words

My wife and I spent the weekend in London, visiting the British Museum, strolling the city centre, having lunch at an Italian restaurant, and shopping for gifts at Hamleys for our boys.

15 words

My wife and I spent the weekend in London, visiting museums, dining, and shopping at Hamleys.

10 words

Went to London with Elisa, visiting museums and shopping.

5 words

London weekend with Elisa, museums, shopping.

Some details goes obviously missing, but the content is still passed on. Depending on circumstances, the receiver of the communication might prefer the crisp and short content of the last message.

Chapter 3

Action, Problem-Solving and Innovation

"You don't have to be great to start, but you have to start to be great" - Zig Ziglar

Strategies are great, until they aren't. Strategies can be a business's most powerful tool, aligning teams, setting the vision, goals and driving success. Yet, even the most well-planned strategies can fall short. When the direction changes, internal disagreements arise, or unforeseen challenges emerge, a company's strategy can quickly become outdated. This is why it's crucial for businesses to constantly evaluate and adapt their strategies to stay ahead of the ever-changing business landscape. To keep up with the pace of change, businesses need to be agile and open to new ideas. This means not only creating a clear and concise strategy, but also fostering a culture of continuous improvement and innovation. This can be achieved by promoting cross-functional collaboration, encouraging diverse perspectives, and rewarding risk-taking and experimentation. By doing so, businesses can empower their teams to think outside the box and come up with creative solutions to the challenges they face. In the end, a business's strategy is only as good as the people who execute it. By providing a supportive environment, businesses can tap into the collective knowledge and skills of their employees, leveraging their strengths and overcoming their weaknesses. When done right, this can lead to a dynamic and resilient organization that is able to navigate any obstacles in its path and achieve its goals.

However, a dilemma arises when strategy becomes the main focus, overshadowing the small daily victories. It can lead to an excessive emphasis on long-term goals, causing mishaps or misfortunes in the short term. Let's remember this relatively funny quote: "In the long run, we are all dead", a quote by John Maynard Keynes that appears in his 1923 work A Tract on Monetary Reform

"We have one strategy: get s**t done". This other quote emerges during training courses, each time with a different author, check it yourself online. In today's world, the pressure to get things done quickly and efficiently is greater than ever before. Companies are constantly striving to stay ahead of the curve and outshine their competition. However, as John Maynard Keynes famously stated, "In the long run, we are all dead". This quote serves as a reminder that while it is important to focus on the present and get things done, we must also keep an eye on the future and ensure that our actions are sustainable in the long term. This is where the second quote, "We have one strategy: get s**t done" comes into play. This is a common phrase used to motivate individuals to take action and achieve their goals. However, it is crucial for company leaders to not only focus on getting things done, but also to ensure that everyone is working towards the same end goal. The danger here is that if everyone is pulling in different directions, the company's efforts may become disjointed and ultimately lead to failure. Therefore, it is important for company leadership to constantly monitor and evaluate the progress of their teams to ensure that everyone is working towards a common goal. This involves effective communication, clear direction, and a shared vision for the future. By doing so, the company can avoid the danger of "stuff getting done" without any real purpose or direction, and instead, focus on achieving long-term success. This quote is very powerful: strategy can take attention away from the now ultimately working against the strategy itself! It's very important that each department of a company has a growth plan with steps lying ahead and that they point in the same direction. But at the end of the day, stuff needs to be done, now.

Having a sales strategy that targets specific markets and clients is highly valuable, but if one spends weeks discussing it in meetings without following through with thirty calls a day, there will be no progress in sales. It is crucial to have a plan in place to ensure a strong, competitive, and reliable portfolio of suppliers, but without consistently seeking out new alternatives and regularly challenging their services and prices, growth and success will not be achieved. A comprehensive strategy for boosting manufacturing over the next seven years can involve acquiring advanced equipment and software in order to enhance productivity and effectiveness. However, if current efforts fail to surpass previous outputs, it can feel like moving backwards despite attempting to progress. The intrapreneur is known for their exceptional drive and ability to achieve results.

There will always be setbacks. Customers expressing dissatisfaction, defective goods, areas for service enhancement. A company is a multifaceted combination of tasks and those who do nothing will achieve perfection.

The saying "Striving for perfection hinders progress" emphasizes that the pursuit of perfection can hinder the implementation of beneficial advancements. Collaborate with colleagues to avoid mistakes, while maintaining a high level of motivation to accomplish tasks. Keep energy high, get stuff done.

The motion of ducks swimming beneath the surface is subtle, easily overlooked. I once met a large business director where everything seemed impeccable but he wasn't shy about mentioning how much fire fighting was going on. As a driven intrapreneur, your goal is for the company to operate like a well-oiled machine, and if it succeeds, it's truly remarkable. Or, is the company not pushing the accelerator hard enough? Motor racing serves as a prime example: the drivers possess incredible talent, yet they often veer off course or crash into barriers. Why does this occur? It is because they are constantly pushing the boundaries of their abilities! However, this cannot be used as a justification for having a fire fighting mentality in your company. Rather, it is important to examine the root causes of these incidents and determine if there is a lack of improvement or if the team is driven to constantly push their limits for long-term growth.

We have witnessed the remarkable capabilities of the intrapreneur, who effectively executes tasks and resolves issues. This is achieved in the immediate time frame and with lasting impact. In the fast-paced world of business, time is of the essence. In order to achieve success, companies must be able to constantly adapt and improve. However, this constant push for growth can sometimes lead to a lack of improvement. When this happens, it is important for teams to come together and work towards finding solutions. This often involves a lot of teamwork and brainstorming, as well as the ability to think outside of the box and come up with creative solutions to problems. Within these challenges and obstacles, there is often a standout individual - the intrapreneur. This person is able to effectively execute tasks and resolve issues, not just in the immediate time frame, but also with a lasting impact. The intrapreneur will pull the team together nurturing 'delivery'. This is a valuable skill to have in the multi-faceted business world, where quick fixes are not always enough. The intrapreneur is able to see the bigger picture and make strategic decisions that benefit the company in the long run. They are a crucial asset to any team, especially when faced with difficult challenges that require both short and long term solutions.. The goal is actually innovation.

Innovation is the key element of business. As a result, companies must rely on their team members to think beyond the present and focus on the bigger picture. Strategic decisions must be made in order to ensure long-term success, and this is where the value of innovative thinking comes into play. When faced with challenging obstacles, it is essential to have team members who can provide both short and long term solutions. We operate in a free market, with plenty of competition, using similar suppliers and supplying similar products to similar customers. The free market is a complex and dynamic environment, with competition and innovation driving success. This requires strategic decision-making and creative thinking to stay ahead. As a business, we must constantly be thinking about the bigger picture and making decisions that will ensure long-term success. This is where the value of innovative thinking comes into play. In order to thrive in this environment, it is essential to have team members who are able to provide both short and long-term solutions. This can be especially important when faced with challenging obstacles that require a creative approach. Through innovative thinking, our team can come up with unique and effective solutions that will not only overcome current obstacles but also set us up for future success. As we navigate the competitive landscape of the free market, we must always keep in mind the importance of being forward-thinking and innovative. By focusing on the bigger picture and making strategic decisions, we can stay ahead of the competition and ensure long-term success. With a team that is able to provide both short and long-term solutions, we can overcome any challenges that come our way and continue to grow and thrive in the free market. Only an unrelentless pace to stay ahead of the competition even for a short while justifies the business existence.

This is where innovation truly shines. Innovation is the driving force behind any successful business. It allows companies to stay ahead of the competition, adapt to changing market trends, and provide unique solutions to customer needs. Without innovation, companies risk becoming stagnant and falling behind their competitors. This is where the importance of having team members who can think outside the box and come up with new ideas comes into play. These individuals are crucial assets to any team, as they bring fresh perspectives and ideas that can lead to long-term success. In the constantly evolving business world, innovation is the key to staying ahead of the game. Only an unrelentless pace to stay ahead of the competition even for a short while justifies the business existence.

The word innovation is often associated with technical wonders like a performing car, a new energy source, the latest electronic gadget, an airplane, a spacecraft. This puts normal people off tracks. Most innovations are process related and not product related. By far most of them don't end up in breakthrough solutions that we all learn about after a few years of commercial success. Every single day, it is small and medium-sized enterprises that tirelessly create and shape the economic terrain through their constant quest for innovation. If you can picture a small medium business in the 1990's and now look around, you can certainly assess the so many differences, all due to innovation.

The intrapreneur just innovates, daily.

Innovation is that change applied to the company, in collaboration with colleagues, that improves the business. It can be a new way of receiving sales order, a more efficient method to organise warehouse picks or sales prospecting, a device speeding up an internal process. Innovation is not just key to success, is it a must for survival!

It doesn't need to be transformational and often it doesn't carry the wow factor. Innovation is not just a buzzword for businesses. It plays a crucial role in the success and even survival of a company. In today's rapidly evolving world, businesses must constantly evolve and adapt to stay relevant. This is why receiving sales orders and streamlining warehouse picks are not just administrative tasks, but opportunities to innovate and improve internal processes. With the advancement of technology, there are now devices that can aid in completing these tasks more efficiently. This not only saves time but also reduces human error, making the process more reliable. As a result, the company becomes more organized, which leads to better sales prospecting and ultimately, a more successful business. Innovation doesn't have to be a grand, groundbreaking idea. It can simply be small improvements made over time that accumulate and lead to a more efficient and successful company. This is why intrapreneurs, or employees who act like entrepreneurs within the company, are crucial. They are the ones who take the initiative to implement these innovative improvements, and eventually, contribute to the overall success of the company.

The relentless pursuit of innovation is what sets successful businesses apart. It is the lifeblood that keeps companies alive, adapting, and thriving in an ever-changing market. This is where the intrapreneur steps in, a key player in any organization. They are the ones who initiate change, who are driven by an unwavering desire to improve and an exceptional ability to execute. Intrapreneurs are the innovators, the game-changers, and the problem solvers. They possess a unique talent for seeing beyond the present, identifying areas for improvement, and implementing creative solutions. It is their daily innovations, those small but powerful changes, that compound over time, creating a ripple effect of success. Like a well-oiled machine, they work tirelessly to ensure the company stays on course, pushing boundaries, and achieving short-term wins while keeping an eye on the long-term vision. But it is not a solo endeavour. Effective intrapreneurs foster collaboration, bringing together colleagues to brainstorm, exchange ideas, and find solutions. They understand the importance of a shared goal and a cohesive team, working in unison to overcome challenges. It is this combination of individual drive and collective effort that propels a company forward, ensuring its survival and setting it apart from the competition.

These relentless, game-changing smaller innovations carry an awe-inspiring magnitude: the unstoppable force of compound. The term comes from the financial world and is often unknown. Put simply, a 1% improvement daily for 100 days delivers much more overall improvement than a 100% improvement at the 100th day. How come? Basically, that little 1% innovation will deliver its good for 99 days, then the following 1% will be helped by the previous one and, on its own right, will deliver its good for 98 days. And so on. The power of compounding small innovations is incredible over the time.

Innovations can be sparked by ideas, by recurring problems, by visiting similar businesses operations including clients and suppliers and much more. Upon discussion with colleagues, an innovative idea will go through analysis and in depth analysis.

There exists an obstacle to innovation, a lurking assassin known as compromise. At times referred to as 'organizational politics', some individuals may desire to have a voice and represent their department's perspective in regards to an idea for the sake of it. However, intrapreneurs do not follow this approach, as they prioritize the best interest of the entire company with utmost importance. They refrain from participating in such actions and instead place a high value on the overall prosperity of the company. Compromises are frequently presented for consideration, watering down the originality and possibly altering it into a different entity. Intrapreneurs are the backbone of any successful company. They are the ones who prioritize the best interest of the entire company with utmost importance, always striving to make the business vision clear and efficient. They are constantly looking for ways to improve the company's processes and bring competitive advantages that will benefit the organization as a whole. Their role is not just limited to advocating for the company's success, but also ensuring that all actions taken align with the company's values and goals. Intrapreneurs refrain from participating in any actions that may harm the company's reputation or hinder its progress. They understand that the success of the company is dependent on the collective efforts and decisions of every individual, and therefore, they prioritize the overall prosperity of the company above personal gain. However, being an intrapreneur also means making compromises. They understand that not every decision will be perfect and that sometimes, compromises need to be made for the greater good of the company. They are willing to present and consider such compromises, but always with the intention of preserving the company's originality and ensuring that it stays true to its core values. Intrapreneurs are the driving force behind the success of a company, constantly striving for progress while keeping the company's best interest at heart.

Chapter 4

Navigating Business Realities

"In God we trust. All others must bring data." This quote by W. Edwards Deming highlights the importance of data in the modern business world. Gone are the days when decisions were made based on gut feelings or intuition. In today's data-driven society, businesses are expected to back up their decisions with solid data and evidence. This is especially true in industries such as finance, technology, and healthcare where data is even more the backbone of success. Gone are the days where businesses could rely solely on their reputation or brand name. With the rise of technology and social media, customers have access to vast amounts of information and data at their fingertips. This means that businesses must constantly monitor and analyse data to stay ahead of the competition and meet the changing needs of their customers. As the saying goes, "what gets measured, gets managed". In order to succeed, businesses must constantly track and analyse data to make informed and strategic decisions. In conclusion, this quote serves as a reminder that data is the key to success in today's business landscape. In order to thrive and stay ahead of the competition, businesses must embrace data and use it to drive their decisions. This mindset shift towards data-driven decision making has revolutionized the way businesses operate and will continue to be a crucial aspect of success in the future. With the world becoming increasingly data-centric, businesses that fail to adapt and embrace this mindset shift will struggle to survive. Data is now the determining factor in every aspect of business operations, from product development and marketing strategies to financial planning and customer relations. In this data-driven era, the role of the intrapreneur has also evolved. No longer can they rely solely on their gut feelings to make decisions. Instead, they must develop a keen sense of data interpretation and analysis. Data has become the starting point for any business idea, and it also serves as the end point, providing valuable insights and feedback on the success or failure of a decision. In this way, the intrapreneur must constantly be attuned to the data, using it to guide their actions and decisions. In conclusion, the rise of data-driven decision making has revolutionized the way businesses operate and will continue to be a crucial aspect of success in the future. As the world becomes increasingly data-centric, companies must adapt and harness the power of data to stay competitive. The intrapreneur, in turn, must also evolve and develop their data-driven mindset to thrive in this new business landscape. Data is no longer just a tool but a fundamental component of decision making, and those who embrace it will have a significant advantage in the business world.

We live in an age with abundance of data. Extracting data from an ERP, playing with an excel model or getting the help of AI, a huge amount of numbers comes up. It is crucial that the intrapreneur remain focused on the goal and maintain a KISS approach: <u>what is that one number that we are trying to improve?</u> Data analysis can be overwhelming when faced with large amounts of information. Whether it is extracting data from an ERP system, working with excel models, or utilizing AI technology, the sheer amount of numbers can be daunting.

To stay on track and achieve our goal, it is crucial to maintain a KISS (Keep It Simple, Stupid) approach. This means focusing on the one number that we are striving to improve. However, it's not just about plugging in formulas and manipulating data. We must also have a clear understanding of the data itself. A spreadsheet with 5 columns and 500 rows of numbers is meaningless without proper context and interpretation. This is where the role of the intrapreneur becomes crucial. They must be able to make sense of the data and identify the key metrics that will drive success. In today's data-driven world, it's not just about gathering numbers, but also about analyzing and understanding them. The successful intrapreneur possesses the vision to grasp the overarching concept and pinpoint the key metric that authentically conveys the narrative. By keeping things simple and staying focused on the goal, they can effectively utilize data to drive business decisions and achieve success.

In a typical financial dataset, it is evident that the term "profit" holds utmost significance in the P&L statement. The focus is on the "invoiced" top line when it comes to sales performance. and in stock management it will be "value in stock". However, these are exceedingly apparent and will not be useful to a sales manager seeking to analyse their client base or purchasing patterns, or to a company looking to reduce inventory in order to enhance cash flow. In so many instances I am submitted documents with too much data so that the story to be portrayed is lost, and the actions recommended for improvement get dispersed or lack focus. The message in these cases is sent on an email without a precise subject, without the interpretation, without the precise the request and the data miss the summary, its meaning. The intrapreneur's ability to simplify data and identify key performance indicators (KPIs) allows for a clearer understanding of the situation at hand. This not only helps to streamline decision-making processes, but also ensures that the recommended actions are both focused and effective. By reducing the amount of data, the intrapreneur is able to highlight the important details and tell a more compelling story. This, in turn, enables the company to make informed decisions and take targeted actions to improve their base or purchasing patterns. Moreover, the intrapreneur's expertise can be particularly beneficial for companies looking to reduce inventory in order to enhance their cash flow. By analysing the data and identifying areas for improvement, the intrapreneur can help the company develop a more efficient inventory management system. This can lead to a reduction in excess stock and a more streamlined supply chain, ultimately resulting in improved cash flow. With a simplified and focused approach, the intrapreneur's recommendations are more likely to be implemented and yield positive results for the company's bottom line. In conclusion, the intrapreneur plays a crucial role in driving organizational success by simplifying complex data and providing actionable insights. Their ability to extract meaningful information from overwhelming amounts of data not only helps companies improve their base or purchasing patterns, but also enables them to make more informed decisions and ultimately enhance their cash flow. By presenting a more concise and focused picture, the intrapreneur empowers companies to take targeted actions and achieve their desired goals.

Business is a balancing act between resources deployed to make products and services available and clients' satisfaction from such products and services. Along the journey, profit and cash must be produced, to warrant the long term standing of the business and the capability to invest in innovation and grow the company. It is a very challenging balance to strike, while customers will often ask more for less and a destructive spiral may initiate. The intrapreneur always focuses on this balance and deploy actions and recommends innovations that favour this balance forward.

Imagine you're running a café. At rush hour, some customers complain because there is a line. The obvious solution can be hiring more baristas, maybe buy an extra coffee machine. But no barista will accept to work an hour a day, and the coffee machine will lie there unused for the rest of the opening hours. What would you do? In every business, things can be improved by deploying resources, but will the profitable equilibrium be unbalanced?

Working in a company can feel like a wild ride, with ups and downs that range from critical client feedback to glowing reviews, and from losing a major order to securing a new contract. It's a constant cycle of setbacks and triumphs. Depending on the company's nature and business strategy, a single success can compensate for multiple failures, while a single failure can put an end to a long line of accomplishments.. In business, it is not uncommon for companies to experience ups and downs. In fact, it's quite the norm. One day, a company can lose a major order and the next day, secure a new contract. This constant cycle of setbacks and triumphs can be quite challenging, requiring companies to maintain a strict approach towards them. This is where intrapreneurs come in. These are individuals within a company who take on an entrepreneurial mindset. They are constantly observing and learning from the failures and celebrating the successes. They understand that, depending on the company's nature and business strategy, a single success can make up for multiple failures. On the other hand, a single failure can have severe consequences and put an end to a long line of accomplishments. For this reason, intrapreneurs must have a strong understanding of the company's goals and strategies. They must be able to navigate through the highs and lows, always keeping the bigger picture in mind. This approach allows companies to continuously improve and strive towards success, even in the face of failures. In this way, intrapreneurs play a crucial role in the overall success of a company. They will learn from fails and celebrate successes.

'Insanity is doing the same thing over and over again and expecting different results'. This sentence of unknown origin strikes a cord around fails: the immediate learning is that very likely the team needs to perform something differently. The company culture will encourage learning from fails as the team understands the importance of gaining new insights and improving. With this mindset, the team will gather and brainstorm ways to turn the fail into a success. The sentence mentioned above is an ever-present reminder that the team can only expect different results by making different choices. This approach will bring about innovation and progress for the company. It is crucial to note that the team will also celebrate successes to acknowledge the hard work, dedication and commitment that has gone into achieving the goal. Celebrating successes will boost team morale, create a positive work environment and motivate the team to achieve more. This practice will also highlight the fact that the company appreciates and values its team members. The team will feel fulfilled and motivated to continue doing their best, which will further the company's growth and success. The team's attitude towards failures and successes will shape the company's culture and determine its future. The team will learn from the past and use the lessons to create a better future for the company. With every failure and success, the team will grow and evolve, leading the company towards success and innovation. The company will thrive on the continuous learning and improvement mindset, creating a culture of progress and success.

Do you believe you are experiencing failure? Do you sense a pattern of repeating mistakes? Sometimes it may help if you <u>duplicate in a "double self"</u>, and watch you performing your tasks, possibly doing mistakes, getting out of the current incumbency. Watch yourself. What's going on around you? Do you have a situational awareness? Are you missing something? Sometimes it can be difficult to identify a problem in your own work. This is why it can be helpful to create a double self and watch yourself performing your tasks. By doing this, you may be able to see where you are making mistakes and how you can improve. It's important to have a sense of situational awareness and to pay attention to what is going on around you. This can help you identify any issues that may be causing you to make mistakes. As you watch yourself, try to be objective and critical. Look for patterns in your mistakes and try to understand why they are happening. This can help you develop strategies to avoid making the same errors in the future. Additionally, by discussing your performance with your line manager, you can gain valuable insight and feedback on how to improve. Your manager will be interested in hearing your thoughts and can offer guidance on how to increase your efficiency and accuracy. Remember to stay on track and know when to end your self-evaluation. Don't get caught up in over-analysing every mistake, as this can lead to a lack of progress. Use your observations to make positive changes and then move on. By continuously monitoring your own performance and seeking feedback, you can avoid repeating mistakes and ultimately improve your overall work performance. It's a concept of developing situational awareness and self-reflection to avoid doing mistakes or simply improve as an intrapreneur.

Enduring through the company's journey and positively adding to its successes and challenges will elevate you to become a valuable intrapreneur, highly valued by the organization. Being a dedicated employee and persevering through the ups and downs of a company's journey can bring great success. It's not just about being a part of the organization, but actively contributing to its growth and overcoming obstacles. This determination and resilience will not only benefit the company, but also elevate you as an intrapreneur, highly valued by the organization. Being an intrapreneur means taking ownership of your role and actively seeking out opportunities for innovation and improvement within the company. This requires the courage to continue moving forward, despite the possibility of failure. By embracing this mindset, you become a valuable asset to the company, constantly pushing for progress and driving positive change. This ongoing dedication and commitment to growth will ultimately lead to the success of both the company and yourself. As the years go by, the accumulations of knowledge will pile up higher and higher, reaching new peaks.

The seasoned intrapreneur, having extensive tenure in the company, is fully immersed in the corporate culture and familiar with all aspects of the company's dynamics. In addition to increasing the success of the company, these accumulations of knowledge also greatly contribute to the personal growth of the intrapreneur. With each passing year, the intrapreneur's skills and abilities will continue to expand and develop, ultimately leading to higher levels of success and achievement. One of the key factors in the success of a seasoned intrapreneur is their extensive tenure within the company. This allows the intrapreneur to become fully immersed in the corporate culture and gain a deep understanding of all aspects of the company's dynamics. This knowledge and experience are invaluable in helping the intrapreneur navigate through various challenges and obstacles, ultimately leading to the success of both the company and themselves.

Another crucial aspect is the ability of the intrapreneur to continually innovate and adapt to changing circumstances. As the knowledge and expertise of the intrapreneur increase, so does their ability to come up with new and innovative solutions to problems. This not only benefits the company but also allows the intrapreneur to constantly improve and develop their skills, leading to even greater success in the future. With each new challenge, the intrapreneur's capabilities will continue to compound, ultimately reaching new peaks of success. Intrapreneurs bring new and innovative solutions to problems, benefiting the company and fostering their own personal growth. The constant challenges they face allow them to develop and refine their skills, laying a foundation for even greater success in the future. With each new obstacle, the intrapreneur's abilities compound, leading them to reach new heights of achievement.

Moreover, the company truly values intrapreneurs who have spent years working and gaining experience within the company. These individuals have lived through the ups and downs of the business, learning from both their failures and successes. As a result, they have a deep understanding of the company's operations and are able to offer unique and valuable perspectives on problem-solving. This makes them highly valuable assets to the company, as they are able to utilize their experience to drive growth and innovation. Intrapreneurs not only benefit the company through their contributions, but also continue to grow and evolve as professionals. Their experiences and successes allow them to build a strong foundation of skills and knowledge, making them valuable assets to any organization. This combination of personal and professional development ultimately leads to a successful and fulfilling career for the intrapreneur. As they continue to face new challenges and overcome obstacles, their capabilities will continue to expand, making them an integral part of the company's continuous growth and success.

Winston Churchill, "Success is not final, failure is not fatal: It is the courage to continue that counts," is a powerful statement about perseverance, resilience, and the ongoing nature of both success and failure.

Chapter 5

Working in the Modern World

The business prides itself in delivering an exceptional offering for clients. Their commitment to quality can be seen through their extensive literature and well-crafted websites. The team works cohesively, leveraging on each other's strengths and delivering great products and services. The culture of collaboration and cooperation is deeply ingrained in their work ethics, leading to a seamless experience for their clients. Furthermore, the business constantly strives to improve and innovate its offerings. Through rigorous market research and customer feedback, they continuously refine their products and services to better meet the needs and expectations of their clients. The team is always open to new ideas and suggestions, welcoming different perspectives to drive growth and progress. This dedication to improvement is what sets them apart and makes them a highly sought-after business in the industry. With a strong foundation of teamwork and a constant drive for improvement, the business has gained a strong reputation for delivering exceptional results. Their clients trust them to provide top-notch products and services, and the business continuously exceeds expectations. As they continue to expand their offerings and reach, the team remains committed to their core values of quality, collaboration, and innovation.

The business have a long standing reputation for being a leader in their field, providing nothing but the best products and services combination in the market. This has been a core value of the company since its inception and has helped them gain the trust of their clients. The team is constantly striving to exceed expectations and deliver exceptional results. The company has continued to grow and expand their offerings, reaching new heights and gaining a larger customer base. Despite this growth, the team remains committed to their core values of quality, collaboration, and innovation. These values are ingrained in every aspect of the business and are the driving force behind their success. Having a strong mission statement and core values is crucial for any business to thrive, and this is evident in the success of this company. Their commitment to quality, collaboration, and innovation has not only gained them a strong reputation, but has also allowed them to continuously exceed the expectations of their clients. As they continue to expand and evolve, these core values will remain at the heart of everything they do.

Let's assume the above is a scenario corresponding to your employment scenario... how do you see your intrapreneur's motive within the company?

More crucially, <u>what is your 'why'?</u>

What motivates you to get up in the morning, head to your job, and exceed the expectations of your coworkers, customers, and stakeholders?

Many people believe that money is the ultimate motivator, but this is not always the case. While it may be a factor, it is not enough to sustain long-term motivation and drive. In fact, studies have shown that having a strong 'why' or purpose is far more important for overall satisfaction and success in both personal and professional life. This is why it is crucial to understand what truly motivates you. Your 'why' is the underlying reason for your actions and behaviours. It is what gets you out of bed in the morning and keeps you going when times get tough. It is the driving force behind your decisions and goals. Without a clear understanding of your 'why', you may find yourself feeling unfulfilled and lacking direction. It is important to take the time to reflect on what truly motivates you and align your actions with your purpose. Only then will you be able to achieve your full potential and make a meaningful impact.

As an entrepreneur, dedicating long hours to my business, I do not view money as the ultimate goal. Instead, it is the lasting legacy of the brand that has been established for over 60+ years. To me, it is both an honour and an exciting challenge to employ exceptional individuals and contribute to their livelihoods. What about you, what is your why?

While it can be challenging to articulate your motives, doing so can greatly benefit both yourself and the organization. This approach can have a profound and lasting impact.

It can be challenging to open up about your motivations, but doing so can have a profound impact on both yourself and the organization. By sharing your why with your line manager, the company director or HR, you can work together to align your personal goals with the company's vision. This allows the company to cater to your individual needs instead of relying on a one-size-fits-all approach. Being able to articulate your why also shows that you are committed to personal growth and development. When your goals and values are aligned with the organization's, you are more likely to be engaged and motivated to perform at your best. This leads to a win-win situation, where both the individual and the company benefit from a harmonious relationship. So, don't be afraid to share your why and see how it can positively impact your career and the company as a whole.

As a business grows and hires more employees, it becomes challenging to maintain close relationships with everyone and fully grasp each individual's personal circumstances. This can lead to a disconnect between the company and its employees, potentially causing disengagement and a lack of motivation. It is crucial for both parties to be on the same page and have a clear understanding of each other's goals and motivations to foster a harmonious relationship. Sharing your "why" with your employer can lead to a win-win situation. By openly communicating your personal motivations and goals, you can create a sense of purpose and fulfilment in your work, which can ultimately lead to increased engagement and motivation. Additionally, this transparency can help your employer better understand your needs and support you in achieving your goals, resulting in a more productive and satisfied workforce. It is beneficial to not only focus on the financial aspects when engaging in business, but also to uncover the underlying motivations for staying with a particular company. This will greatly benefit the HR department and further elevate the company's reputation as one that truly values its employees.

SMEs are known for their close-knit work environments, where employees often form strong personal connections with each other and the company. This is due in part to the flat organizational structure commonly adopted by SMEs, which allows for easier communication and a sense of cohesion within the company. This structure also fosters a more collaborative work culture, where everyone from the owners to the directors and colleagues are working towards a common goal. In addition to the benefits of communication and cohesion, the flat organizational structure of SMEs also allows for a more agile and adaptable workforce. With fewer layers of hierarchy, decisions can be made and implemented quickly, without the red tape often found in larger companies. This flexibility is especially beneficial in today's business landscape, where the ability to pivot and adapt to changing circumstances is crucial for success. Moreover, this type of organizational structure also enables SMEs to create a more inclusive and transparent work environment. With fewer layers between management and employees, everyone has a voice and can contribute to the company's growth and success. This not only boosts employee morale and satisfaction, but also helps to attract and retain top talent, further elevating the company's reputation as a desirable place to work. Ultimately, the flat organizational structure of SMEs has numerous benefits, not just in terms of financial success, but also in creating a positive and thriving work culture.

My door is always open according to my MD policy. You can visit me anytime and I will make myself available. If I am not present, please utilize emails or other forms of communication and I will respond at the earliest possible time. However, it is important to consider the reason for seeing me, or any other colleague. Some time back, I posted a notice on my door requesting colleagues to come and see me only when they were ready, with well-defined concepts. First and foremost, make sure the problem is clearly understood, then consider the various approaches we can take to address it, and finally, suggest the most suitable solution. In discussions, I enjoy reiterating that we are likely familiar with all the issues plaguing our business, often repeating "knowing the problems is the easy bit". However, the remedies and their execution may be eluding us or still out of our grasp. Hence, the request is to ensure effective communication and bear in mind that the intrapreneur's role is not solely relaying messages, but also enhancing their significance.. Door is open, keep it simple: describe the problem of opportunity, list down our options, then confirm what you recommend we do. My answer will often be "yes, go ahead and well done".

We have reached the pivotal moment: frequently, a profession is misinterpreted as merely completing assignments. Indeed, it is undeniable that throughout our daily routine, we inevitably have a multitude of tasks to complete, whether they be mundane or novel in nature. Energy is essential for the generation of results. Your brain and personality are the key to propelling both yourself and your business towards success. In this accelerated environment, we are constantly bombarded with tasks and assignments that need to be completed. As a result, many people often view their profession as a means to an end, where the goal is to simply get the job done. However, as an intrapreneur, one's role is not limited to simply completing assignments. In fact, it goes far beyond that.

As we go about our day, it's important to remember that the door to opportunity is always open. By keeping things simple, we can effectively describe problems and opportunities, list down our options, and confirm what we recommend we do. This approach helps reaching a pivotal moment, where the intrapreneur can truly make a difference in their profession. It allows to break free from the monotony of completing tasks and instead, focus on creating meaningful impact. As an intrapreneur, it's crucial to understand that our role is not just about completing tasks, but also about seizing opportunities and creating positive change. Our work should not be misinterpreted as a mundane routine, but rather as a platform to showcase our innovative thinking and problem-solving skills. By embracing this mindset, we can truly make a difference and become intrapreneurs who are constantly pushing boundaries and making a lasting impact in our profession.

Fifty years ago, businesses would hire workers to operate typewriters in order to produce well-written letters. At that moment, managing the influx and outflow of correspondence post was a real job! Presently, we independently compose, transmit, and obtain communications without any outside assistance, it is difficult to this that managing the post was actually a job. This example clearly indicates the dominance of technology and innovation, resulting in the disappearance of these tasks and the transformation of the jobs landscape. The advancement of technology will inevitably alter the terrain, duties will evolve, yet a corporation will eternally require intellectual capacity. The dominance of technology has led to significant changes in the modern workplace. The intrapreneur sees a huge opportunity in technology to shift their contribution to the business from mundane tasks to the value of ideas and innovation. With the help of technology, employees can now focus on using their intellectual capacity to come up with innovative solutions and strategies to drive the business forward. This shift in focus has not only improved the quality of work but has also opened up new opportunities for employees to grow and thrive in their roles. As technology continues to evolve, it will inevitably alter the terrain of the workplace. Duties will continue to evolve and change, but one thing that will remain constant is the need for human intellect. A corporation will always require individuals who can think critically, come up with new ideas, and adapt products and services to changing circumstances. The role of the intrapreneur will continue to be crucial in driving the success of businesses, and technology will only enhance their ability to do so.

The ever-changing landscape of work will once again be revolutionized by the advent of AI. Just as computers and printers supplanted typewriter operators, and emails took over post management, AI will revolutionize the landscape even further. AI technology is becoming increasingly prevalent in businesses, and its success is a testament to its potential. With the help of AI, businesses are able to optimize their operations and increase productivity. This ultimately leads to more success, allowing businesses to thrive in today's competitive market. As AI continues to evolve and improve, this success will only continue to grow. AI's impact on businesses goes beyond just boosting success. It will also have a significant effect on the way we work. The introduction of AI will bring about a new era of work, one that is more efficient and innovative. This will allow workers to shift their focus from mundane and repetitive tasks to more creative and strategic work. As a result, employees will have more time to dedicate to innovation, ultimately leading to a more dynamic and progressive work environment.

However, it goes beyond this. I am of the belief that my co-workers are present due to their intelligence and their methods in dealing with business affairs. If AI were to solely handle tasks, it could potentially displace humans, much as computers did with typewriters. Being an intrapreneur, you undoubtedly employ your intellect to generate meaningful contributions to the company's success.

When commencing your employment, there will have been an agreement in place outlining your job responsibilities. As time progresses, the duties and responsibilities outlined in the job description will have undergone transformation, most likely resulting in modifications to the contract as well. These are essential for adhering to legal requirements and serving as a guiding light in the event of any confusion. One intriguing aspect of these entities is their operational schedule, typically adhering to the conventional timeframe of 9 to 5. The prevalence of modern technologies has sparked a shift in the way we communicate, followed by the revolutionary idea of remote work.

Policymakers are also taking steps towards implementing measures to safeguard the employee's right to disconnect, ensuring that they are not obligated to respond to work-related communication outside of their designated working hours. This is completely just and will undoubtedly make a difference in situations where the customary availability of non-negotiated hours is ceaseless and disquieting.

I am not a legal expert and have not thoroughly studied these laws, but as an employer, my perspective is based on practicality and my goal of ensuring the success of the business, intrapreneurs and all colleagues. It is relatively simple to allocate a specific time period for various tasks involved in running a business: for instance, when utilizing a machine, one must be present at the machine; when utilizing a laptop, one can turn it on and off at will; and when using a phone, one has the option to silence it and disregard incoming calls. The divide between upholding an individual's personal time and ensuring a seamless workflow for the organization and its members, in the deepest meaning of "company", is already a murky territory within these work tasks.

The idea of living two separate lives, one personal and one professional, is a notion that cannot be universally accepted. Our existence is a blend of individual and professional aspects, including familial, athletic, leisure, commercial, and creative pursuits, depending on our roles and responsibilities. Our contributions to the company's success are not limited to our professional lives. In fact, our personal lives play a significant role in shaping who we are and how we approach our work. It is the combination of our individual and professional aspects that make us unique and valuable to the company. As we navigate through our various roles and responsibilities, we bring with us a diverse set of skills and experiences from our familial, athletic, leisure, commercial, and creative pursuits. These aspects of our lives are not separate from our professional lives, but rather they are intertwined and complement each other. Each one of us humans, is a one whole person. Our efforts, creativity, ethics, and modus operandi remain consistent across all aspects of our single life, allowing us to excel in all areas. In a society where there is often a pressure to compartmentalize our lives, it is important to recognize the value of living a holistic life. By embracing all aspects of our lives, we can bring a well-rounded perspective to our work and contribute to the success of the company. Our individuality is what makes us stand out and by integrating all aspects of our single life, we can truly thrive both personally and professionally. We have one life, there's no switch between characters.

The switch is only the clock when we allocate time to tasks. We each have the power to govern our minds, determining what to ponder. While we may naturally focus on work during business hours, personal interests or hobbies may also surface throughout the day, which is completely acceptable.

The concept of the right to disconnect seems flawed to me in this context. It solely revolves around tasks that are vulnerable to automation, neglecting other important aspects of work. Our mind is a singular entity, experiencing one existence. It remains constantly active, absorbing knowledge from all sources and at all times, sparking thoughts on every aspect of our existence, regardless of the time of day or night. The innovative intrapreneur generates concepts to be executed in the workplace at all hours, perhaps even during the night! At any point in one's life, the mind will make connections between dots and generate ideas that can be put to use in a professional setting. Why should we not write a note about a good idea that came outside of 'working hours'? Is it an invasion of our private lives? Mine is a simple a reflection of our human nature!

Throughout my usual routine, I have been struck with innovative concepts at any given moment - whether it be during weekdays, weekends, or while on holiday! Has this experience occurred to you as well? While transferring the yogurt from its packaging into a glass, observing my child engaged in sports, strolling through the streets during a pub crawl, mounting a picture frame, and organizing the loft or the garage... My mind was often sparked with business ideas, just to mention a handful. If an intrapreneur or employee experiences this, should they reject the idea and attempt to rewire and erase their thoughts because it occurred outside of their designated work hours?

The forward-thinking intrapreneur utilizes technology to complete tasks promptly and effectively, all while maintaining an inquisitive mindset towards living a fulfilling life.

Remote working (work from home) has become a popular reality after the pandemic, yet again, helped by technology. The concept has gained significant traction in recent years, prompting major corporations to adopt divergent stances – with some advocating for it and others opposing it. Regarded as a high-end benefit, it is a privilege not accessible to everyone; coworkers operating specialized equipment, stocking shelves in a store, caring for patients in a clinic, or supervising teams transporting goods in a warehouse are unable to commute.

At my current workplace, work from home is not an option for the majority of employees. Despite the recent trend of remote work, only one position is deemed eligible for this privilege. This decision is justified by the limited availability of office facilities, which is why most of the workforce, both in the factory and the office, come to work on a daily basis. This allows for face-to-face interactions and fosters a sense of teamwork among employees. Additionally, being in close proximity to the products and processes allows for a better understanding of the company's operations. The decision to limit work from home also ensures that employees are able to build relationships with their colleagues. By physically being present in the workplace, employees have the opportunity to meet and interact with their coworkers, creating a strong sense of camaraderie. This is especially important for effective collaboration and problem-solving within teams.

Furthermore, being in the same space as other teams and the products themselves allows for a better understanding of the company's goals and objectives, leading to increased productivity and satisfaction among employees. While working from home may be a convenient option for some, the benefits of being physically present in the workplace far outweigh the limitations.

The definition of a company has been previously outlined, and it is this very idea that draws us to the assembly of individuals in a physical space. Effective communication goes beyond the limitations of email, messaging, and even video calls. While attending the office, flash meetings can be organised, serendipity chats can spark anytime anywhere, and a rapport between people will build. The bond that forms from one-to-one interactions, progressing to one-to-two, and eventually to one-to-many, is instrumental in creating a company and its culture. It serves as a dynamic force that embraces failure and strives for continuous success.

The digital age has brought about a new era of communication, where chats can spark anytime, anywhere. These spontaneous interactions between individuals are the foundation for building a strong rapport. As people continue to engage in one-to-one chats, relationships form and strengthen. This connection, however small, has the power to expand to one-to-two and eventually to one-to-many interactions. This evolution is not only crucial for individuals but also plays a vital role in creating a company and its culture. The bond formed through these chats serves as a dynamic force within a company. It fosters an environment that embraces failure and encourages continuous success. As individuals connect and share ideas, they create a sense of camaraderie and trust within the organization. This, in turn, leads to a culture that values collaboration and open communication. Working together towards a common goal becomes second nature, and the company thrives as a result. However, in today's world, where working from home is often seen as a privilege, the opportunities of the intrapreneur may be jeopardized. Without the physical presence of colleagues and the spontaneous chats that come with it, building relationships and creating a strong company culture may prove to be challenging. This is where the power of virtual communication tools, such as chats, comes into play. These tools allow for the same level of connection and rapport building, even in a remote work setting. As long as the company values and encourages these virtual interactions, the bond between individuals and the strength of the company's culture can continue to thrive, regardless of physical distance.

A company thrives when all its elements are pushing towards the same direction, and when this sentiment pervades the business. It remains crucial though that every individual brings to the table their own ideas and suggestions. This can happen during any type of meeting, which, as we saw before, the intrapreneur will organise with a clear attendee list, duration, outcome to achieve. However, these is a particular kind of meeting that necessitates an immediate termination,: the one in which all are in immediate agreement. This statement may incite controversy, but if everyone is immediately in consensus and there are no further contributions to the topic, was the meeting a waste of everyone's time? While reflecting on this, we shall ask ourselves: how is it possible that all agree on something instantly? Maybe someone couldn't speak out? This is a delicate situation because no one wants to be the sole person causing disruption and creating controversy. Some colleagues may refrain from voicing their opinions and this will lead to a lack of diverse perspectives, to the detriment of the business, it can ultimately hinder progress and growth within a team or an entire organization. Therefore, it is essential to create a safe and open environment where individuals feel comfortable expressing their thoughts and opinions, even if they may differ from the majority. This guarantees a well-rounded and comprehensive decision-making process. In conclusion, while immediate consensus may seem like the ideal scenario, it is important to recognize that there may be underlying factors preventing individuals from fully participating in the discussion. As such, it is crucial to encourage and value diverse perspectives and to not dismiss the possibility of further contributions, even if everyone seems to be in agreement. By doing so, we can ensure that all voices are heard and that the best possible outcome is achieved. It's a business environment, remember, and colleagues will be all there to get to the best decision.

A bit like "we've always done it this way", which we all know is a forbidden sentence in business. In the meeting, everyone seemed to be in agreement, with no one voicing any challenges or concerns. It was as if the meeting was just going through the motions and no one wanted to rock the boat. This lack of dissent and in-depth analysis was not only a waste of time, but it also gave off a sense of company politics at play. It was almost as if everyone was afraid to speak up and risk going against a superior colleague. This type of environment can be dangerous and counterproductive for a business. Silence can be just as damaging as agreeing with something you don't truly believe in. When one individual chooses to remain silent, it can give the impression of agreement with a superior colleague. This can create an unhealthy power dynamic and stifle open communication within the team. It's important for everyone to feel comfortable voicing their opinions and concerns in a meeting, even if it goes against the popular opinion.

<u>The intrapreneur always speaks out, consistently constructively</u>.

This is how growth and progress can be achieved. Furthermore, the phrase "we've always done it this way" is often frowned upon in the business world. It shows a lack of willingness to adapt and try new things. In a meeting where this mindset prevails, it can be difficult to have productive discussions and come up with innovative ideas. It's important for individuals to challenge the status quo and offer different perspectives, even if it goes against what has been done in the past. This is how companies can continue to evolve and stay ahead in a competitive market.

"Your work is going to fill a large part of your life, and the only way to be truly satisfied is to do what you believe is great work"

Steve Jobs

Chapter 6

Personal Development and Professional Growth

The quote "If all you have is a hammer, everything looks like a nail" is attributed to Abraham Maslow and is an example of the law of the instrument, also known as Maslow's hammer or the golden hammer. The quote refers to the cognitive bias of over-relying on a familiar tool, which can lead to approaching problems in unhelpful or destructive ways.

The quote is often used to illustrate the idea that people tend to use the tools they're familiar with, even when better options might be available. For example, in health and nutrition, the "diet hammer" is the idea that a perfect diet is the answer to all health problems.

There are many ways to interpret this quote and apply it to our own lives. As we go through our daily routines, we often rely on the tools and habits that we are familiar with, even if there may be better options available to us. This can be seen in various aspects of our lives, from our diet and exercise habits to the way we approach problem-solving. When we expand this quote to ourselves, we may realize that we have multiple "hammers" in our lives - different areas where we rely on familiar tools or habits, even if they may not be the most effective. By recognizing this, we can become more open-minded and willing to try new approaches and tools, leading to growth and improvement in various aspects of our lives. Remembering this quote can serve as a reminder to continuously evaluate and challenge our habits and thoughts, and to not be afraid to let go of the old hammers and try out new ones.

Your toolset is undoubtedly a vast arsenal at your disposal, utilized on a daily basis. This set of tools essentially encompasses your skills set. This is excellent material because it enables you to achieve remarkable outcomes in your life as an intrapreneur, and embodies a transformative approach. Have you ever considered the lack of resources at your disposal? Imagine having a manual screwdriver and using it every day to tighten screws, without ever coming across an electric screwdriver or wondering if anything better than a screwdriver is available.

As an intrapreneur, you are constantly seeking ways to improve and achieve remarkable outcomes in your life. This transformative approach encourages you to expand your skillset and discover new tools that will help you on your journey. With the rapid evolution of technology and the workplace, it is essential to continuously work on improving your skills and knowledge. Imagine having a manual screwdriver as your only tool, and using it every day to tighten screws. While it may get the job done, you will soon realize the limitations and inefficiencies of this approach. This is analogous to only relying on your current skillset and not seeking out new opportunities to expand it. Just like coming across an electric screwdriver, discovering new tools and techniques can greatly enhance your abilities as an intrapreneur. Don't wait until you feel the lack of resources to start expanding your toolset. Take the initiative to continuously learn and grow, and you will see the remarkable outcomes it can bring to your life. Reading books, attending workshops, and seeking out mentors are all valuable ways to expand your skillset and become a more successful intrapreneur. Keeping an open mind and embrace the possibilities that come with expanding your toolset, and you will see the transformative impact it can have on your life.

Successful people read lots of books, and reading can help people achieve success. People, like Jeff Bezos, Warren Buffett, and Elon Musk, read daily. A Harvard study found that top CEOs read up to four books a month. Reading can boost motivation and curiosity, which can lead to a positive trajectory of success. Reading books on a wide range of topics can help people generate innovative solutions to problems.

The intrapreneur proactively addresses the areas in which is aware needs improving on. However, what is even more challenging are unknowns of which is not even aware of being ignorant about. Only through curiosity can we uncover the mysteries.

Curiosity is a basic element of cognition that is related to inquisitive thinking. It can be used to describe a specific behaviour or as a way to explain that behaviour. A BBC study found that participants who reported being more curious tended to have better experiences in their jobs, social relationships, and use of innovation.

Curiosity acts as a catalyst, igniting a desire to acquire knowledge and explore, particularly on subjects that hold personal significance, but also byond them. The intrapreneur's insatiable curiosity fuels an ever-growing understanding of diverse subjects, ultimately propelling them to excel in accomplishing objectives, tackling fresh obstacles, and exceeding all expectations.

Be curious yourself. Demonstrate curiosity by displaying your own inquisitiveness and candor. You do not have to possess all the solutions, and it is acceptable to acknowledge that you do not possess complete knowledge.

Be open-minded and curious to ideas and opinions. Encourage thinking outside the box, to challenge their own biases, and to embrace uncertainty. This will create a safe, open environment where diverse ideas can flow freely. Additionally, being open-minded yourself will set a good example for your team and encourage them to do the same. By cultivating open-mindedness, you will create a team that is not afraid to take risks and explore new possibilities. Moreover, being open-minded will also help your team excel in accomplishing objectives. By being receptive to new ideas, your team will be able to come up with innovative solutions to tackle obstacles and overcome challenges. This will also lead to a more diverse and well-rounded team, as different perspectives and experiences will be taken into consideration. As a leader, it is important to create an environment where everyone feels comfortable sharing their thoughts and ideas. This will lead to a more collaborative and productive team, ultimately exceeding all expectations. In addition, being open-minded also means being willing to admit when you do not have all the answers. It is acceptable to acknowledge that you do not possess complete knowledge and that there may be others who know more about a certain topic. By doing so, you are showing humility and promoting a culture of continuous learning. This will also create an environment where team members feel comfortable asking questions and seeking guidance, leading to personal and professional growth. Ultimately, being open-minded will not only benefit your team's performance, but also create a positive and inclusive work culture.

The crucial way to create a culture of continuous learning is by embracing a growth mindset. Having a growth mindset means being open to new challenges and actively seeking out opportunities for growth. By fostering this mindset within your team, you can encourage a sense of curiosity and a passion for learning. This can lead to team members being more willing to stretch themselves, confront obstacles, and take risks in order to improve and progress. In addition to promoting personal and professional growth, having a growth mindset will also help the intrapreneur to create an inclusive and positive work culture. The intrapreneur encourages team members to embrace a growth mindset, you are promoting a sense of openness and vulnerability. This can lead to team members feeling more comfortable asking questions and seeking guidance from one another, creating a supportive environment where everyone feels valued and heard. Ultimately, embracing a growth mindset can not only benefit individual team members, but also strengthen the overall performance and dynamic of the team.

The pursuit of knowledge stems from an innate curiosity and a willingness to pose unbounded inquiries, which, as previously stated, holds immense influence. This extends further, as it embarks on a voyage of self-improvement across various subjects, broadening one's repertoire and tackling novel challenges and prospects in innovative ways. Undoubtedly, this expedition entails avid perusal and proactive involvement in diverse training and enhancement endeavours.

A lesson that will remain ingrained in my memory was centred on the concept of '<u>causativity</u>'.

The training spanned several days and was triggering some deep thinking, causing a certain level of astonishment among certain attendees, resulting in some of them leaving the program. In essence, it boils down to the notion that there are no justifications: you alone are answerable for everything in your life.

A moment of reflection is required.

Please read it again. Take a moment to contemplate it. And read it again.

Consider your individual existence, your connection with your loved ones, your financial situation, your style of attire, and the nature of your employment. These components are all consequences of your actions. No excuses, it's your merit, or, if you don't like them, your fault. When one fully embraces this mindset, happiness is unleashed to its utmost extreme. There are no irritations, everything is as it is, all because of you.

The typical objection: if I was born from a billionaire, I would drive a better car, experience lavish holidays and my bank account will show many more figures. Well, I will answer with "maybe". If you are reading this book, you weren't born that way. Still, everything else is the result of your actions. You can't do anything to the financial position of your parents when you were born and they grew you up. But you can do a heck of a lot on everything else!

In year 2000 I fell victim of a car crash, a head on collision that I only luckily survived and left most of my bones broken. I wasn't driving and the fault was 100% on the other car. The accident itself was completely away from my sphere of influence. What could I influence? Everything afterwards! Keep smiling, work hard. After surgeries and an year of physiotherapy, I walked properly again. I still can't run, nor walk long distances. That's fine, I did everything I could after an adverse event. No bad feeling, it's how life goes... if anything, I could only be grateful I survived the accident. I endeavoured to maintain authority over my fate by assuming responsibility for the circumstance and exerting every effort within my power.

My personal experience may help you giving the right power to causativity: it's not about the work environment, but life as a whole. The moment you take ownership for everything happening to you and around you coincide with the moment you feel accomplished and happy.

If your personal relationship with a family member or colleague isn't great, being causative doesn't mean simply admitting "it's all my fault." Rather, it's about taking responsibility for being the source of the solution. It's about shifting your mindset to focus on what you can change: how you approach the situation, how you present yourself, and how you adapt your own behaviour to connect with the other person. When you take a causative approach, you stop seeing yourself as a passive participant and instead become an active force for improving the relationship.

Ownership doesn't mean blame—it means understanding that you have the power to reshape any challenging dynamic and unlock a better connection.

Causativity is contagious. When you shift your behaviour and take ownership of a situation, you influence those around you. Your change in approach, your willingness to take responsibility and engage constructively, creates a ripple effect. People start to mirror your actions—often without even realizing it. By becoming the catalyst for positive change, you inadvertently encourage others to adopt the same mindset. They, too, begin to see themselves as the source of solutions, taking ownership of their own actions and interactions. This cycle of causativity doesn't require force or direct persuasion; it's the natural result of leading by example. As you embody the change you seek, you help to cultivate a culture where everyone, together, becomes more proactive, more accountable, and more causative.

The intrapreneur shows high levels of causativity.

Embracing causativity will make a new you. In full ownership of what's around you and your destiny. The feeling is fulfilling and it fits perfectly to the 'forward going', 'go getter', 'this will be sorted' approach of the intrapreneur.

Examples of causativity.

1. You organised a meetup with a friend, but you turn up at the wrong place. The non-causative person then engages with the friend with "you told me to come here but it's incorrect". The causative approach is "I understood it was

here". It is often said that the causative approach take the form of sentences with the own self as a subject, typically starting with "I.... ". It remains obvious that telling your friend "I was told we would meet up here" is not causative, because the subject of the sentence stands as a passive element of the activity.

2. An argument is developing with your partner. The non causative insists on sentenced with "you" as a subject. What is the typical result? The voice tone raises sentence after sentence until the complete closure and a bit of a fallout happens. The causative person steers the conversation, even when it's close to a confrontation, putting the own self as a subject, with sentences starting with "I.... ". In this instance, these sentences will need to remain constructive, they won't be "I am good, I am better, I am nice, I am clever" because they just distance ourselves from other people. They will be more like "I am sorry, I interpreted such behaviour as .... And I will make sure we can understand each other better in future" and "I suggest and I will make sure from now on that for sensitive topics we don't talk randomly while we are busy but we sit down and talk things through properly".

3. At work, something went wrong for a client. The company is researching the root causes of the problem to prevent it from happening again. A meeting between three departments is going on and getting a bit heated. It's often referred to as 'defensive mode' and colleagues start saying what others did wrong. In these cases, the causative intrapreneur can step in, keep the own self as the sentences subject: "I believe my department informed A and B about what needed doing, and I will double check this happened"

and "I suggest next time, when we have similar type of orders, we circulate a precise document with all tasks, prompting it from a video call so we are all up to pace" and "I suppose our system failed somewhere, my department will keep a close eye on similar orders". These would be instead of "your departments A and B didn't read what we wrote" and "You didn't tell me it was going to require such activities from my team" and "you didn't follow the procedures". Albeit the events could actually be the result of some colleagues not reading messages or procedures, insisting on it won't get your leadership further. It can sound frustrating, but only by embracing the issue from 'above', with an intrapreneurial and causative mind will boost your leadership and avoid the problem from happening again.

4. If you're dissatisfied with the holidays you're taking part in, being causative means taking responsibility for improving the situation. Instead of simply accepting things as they are, you can proactively communicate your ideas to your fellow holiday-goers. Work with them to find a destination that fits within a mutually agreeable budget and aligns with your preferences. By taking the initiative to present and advocate for your ideal holiday choice, you help shape the outcome rather than passively waiting for change.

The examples could go on about all aspects in life, even those deepest rooted problems. Causativity, sometimes referred to as 'accountability', projects from the traits of proactivity, but it's deeper, it's about refusing that something is just the way it is, and take responsibility for any lack of changes we desire to happen.

As an intrapreneur, not only will you be in full ownership of what's around you, but you will also be in full control of your destiny. This level of control and responsibility can be daunting for some, but for the intrapreneur it is exhilarating. The feeling of fulfilment that comes with being a causativity champion intrapreneur is unmatched. It is this feeling that motivates them to strive for higher levels of success. Additionally, the intrapreneur's causative nature is what sets them apart from the crowd. They are not content with simply waiting for things to happen, they create the opportunities they desire. This forward-thinking and go-getter attitude perfectly aligns with the intrapreneur's mindset, making them the ideal candidate for success.

To complement all of this, the intrapreneur's manners and appearance must also match their ambitious nature. Dressing for success is not about changing who you are, but rather, it is about dressing to match your individuality and ambitions. Intrapreneurs have a unique ability to combine their personal and professional lives into one. They understand that life is about balance and that success in one area can lead to success in the other. With this mindset, they are able to approach all aspects of life with determination and confidence. This makes them the ideal candidate for success in the business world. In addition to their mindset, intrapreneurs also understand the importance of appearance and manners. They know that first impressions are crucial and that their appearance and demeanour must align with their ambitious nature. This is why they take the time to dress for success. It is not about changing who they are, but rather, it is about dressing in a way that reflects their individuality and goals. By doing so, they are able to project a sense of professionalism and confidence, making them stand out in the business world. Intrapreneurs are in a league of their own. They possess a unique combination of qualities that make them stand out in the workplace. Their ability to balance their personal and professional lives, along with their attention to appearance and manners, sets them apart from the rest. With these traits, they are able to achieve success in all areas of their life and become valuable assets to any organization. In the workplace, it is essential for individuals to possess certain traits that set them apart from others. One such quality is the ability to maintain an engaging presence while conversing with others. This includes maintaining appropriate eye contact and posture, which not only showcases confidence but also displays respect and interest in the conversation. By doing so, one can create a positive impression on their colleagues and superiors, which can prove to be beneficial in the long run. Moreover, having a professional demeanour is crucial in the workplace. This encompasses not only one's appearance but also their manners and behaviour. It is essential to present oneself in a well-groomed manner, as it reflects one's attention to detail and professionalism. Additionally, having good manners and etiquette can go a long way in building strong relationships and fostering a positive work environment. These qualities not only make an individual stand out but also make them a valuable asset to any organization. As professionals, it is important to strike a balance between personal and professional life. This involves managing one's time efficiently and prioritizing tasks accordingly. By doing so, individuals can not only excel in their careers but also maintain a healthy work-life balance. This, in turn, can lead to increased productivity and overall satisfaction in both personal and professional spheres. With the right attitude and a focus on maintaining a well-rounded life, one can achieve success in all areas of their life and contribute positively to their organization.

A healthy work-life balance is crucial for overall satisfaction and productivity. Maintaining a well-rounded life allows individuals to excel in both personal and professional spheres. By prioritizing self-care and setting boundaries, one can achieve success in all areas of their life and positively contribute to their organization. However, achieving this balance requires the right attitude and a conscious effort to avoid overworking. It is vital to remember that success is not just about achieving career goals, but it also includes maintaining healthy relationships, taking time for hobbies and leisure activities, and prioritizing mental and physical well-being. In today's speed oriented society, it is easy to get caught up in the hustle and neglect other aspects of life. However, it is essential to remember that a burnout can hinder productivity and negatively impact one's personal life. Therefore, it is crucial to prioritize self-care and maintain a healthy work-life balance to achieve long-term success. Always remain polite, even in awkward situations, as lashing out never pays back. Instead, staying calm and constructive can lead to better outcomes. Remember to set boundaries and prioritize self-care to maintain a healthy work-life balance. By doing so, you can achieve success in all areas of your life and positively contribute to your organization. Knowing when to stop and take a break is also essential. By balancing work and personal life, you can avoid burnout and achieve long-term success.

Certainly your person at work doesn't behave that much differently to the person on a night out. It's important to maintain a consistent and honourable standing, no matter the setting. Whether you're in a professional environment or enjoying a night out with friends, your behaviour and actions should always align with your values and beliefs. This includes how you present yourself on social media. In today's digital age, it's crucial to remember that what you post online can have a significant impact on your personal and professional reputation. So make sure your social media feeds reflect the same level of integrity and respect that you exhibit in person. Continuously think before you post, and consider how your words and images may be perceived by others. By keeping a mindful and responsible approach to your online presence, you can ensure that your character remains consistent, both in and out of the workplace.

"True success lies not in never failing, but in how we rise after we fall. It's a journey of constant learning, adapting, and staying true to our vision" - Steven Bartlett

Chapter 7

Creating a Legacy and Making an Impact

Becoming an intrapreneur requires both time and effort. Being an intrapreneur is a journey and it takes time to develop the necessary skills. It requires dedication and a consistent work ethic. Successful intrapreneurs are continuously working on themselves, improving their skills, and staying updated on their industry. An intrapreneur is someone who works within an organization to create innovative ideas. Being an intrapreneur is about thinking outside the box, taking risks, and having the courage to challenge the status quo. It's about having the drive and determination to make a difference within the company. This type of mindset requires a lot of energy and effort, but the impact can be significant. Becoming an intrapreneur also means being open to learning and self-improvement. A successful intrapreneur is constantly seeking new knowledge, whether it's through reading, attending workshops, or networking with other professionals. They understand that in order to stay relevant and innovative, they must continuously work on themselves. It's not just about the end result, but the journey and the growth that comes with it. Intrapreneurs are always pushing themselves to be better, and that takes consistent effort and dedication.

An intrapreneur is highly valued and sought after by colleagues, clients, suppliers, stakeholders, friends and family members. This is because they possess a unique set of qualities that make them stand out in a crowd. They are driven, innovative, and constantly pushing themselves to be better. This dedication and determination not only benefits their personal growth, but also positively impacts those around them. Intrapreneurs understand that success is not just about the end result, but also about the journey and the growth that comes with it. This mindset is what sets them apart from the rest. They are not afraid to take risks and think outside the box, constantly challenging the status quo. This allows them to come up with new and innovative ideas that can lead to groundbreaking achievements. Their consistent effort and dedication to self-improvement is what makes intrapreneurs so valuable in today's fast-shifting reality and ever-changing business world. They are constantly adapting to new challenges and finding ways to improve themselves and their work. This not only benefits their own personal growth and development, but also the growth and success of the companies they work for. Intrapreneurs are truly the driving force behind innovation and progress in the professional world.

The growth and development of intrapreneurs is not only beneficial for their own personal and professional growth but also for the companies they work for. They have the ability to adapt to new challenges and find ways to constantly improve themselves and their work. This adaptability and constant drive for improvement is what makes them the driving force behind innovation and progress in the professional world. As intrapreneurs continue to evolve and grow, the company as a whole will also see the positive impact of their transformation. They are always focused on delivering results, never giving up in the face of failure or setbacks. Instead, they simply learn from these experiences and use them to fuel their innovation. This mindset allows them to always be prepared for the next challenge and to celebrate their successes along the way. Intrapreneurs truly embody the qualities of resilience, determination, and adaptability. They are not afraid to take risks and are always looking for ways to improve themselves and their work. Their constant drive for growth and development benefits not only themselves but also the companies they work for, making them an invaluable asset in today's ever-changing professional landscape.

An intrapreneur is always selling: a pleasant character that people likes to deal with in the recurrence of business duties. This selling should be interpreted in its highest value, where the stakeholders are 'clients', not simply 'customers'. It is not just about making a sale or closing a deal, but about building meaningful and lasting relationships with those we work with. An intrapreneur understands the importance of treating stakeholders as valuable clients, not just as faceless customers. They prioritize communication, empathy, and trust, knowing that these qualities are essential for successful collaborations and partnerships. An intrapreneur is constantly seeking ways to enhance the client experience, whether through innovation, problem-solving, or providing exceptional service. They are always looking for opportunities to add value and exceed expectations, because for an intrapreneur, the satisfaction of their clients is the ultimate measure of success.

In today's competitive business landscape, the key to success lies not only in the core products or services a company offers, but also in the quality of their work. This is where intrapreneurs come in - individuals who possess an entrepreneurial mindset and drive within a corporate setting. Whether they hold higher positions of responsibility within a company or work alongside their colleagues, intrapreneurs are constantly selling their work to meet the desired quality set by the client. The term "client" here can refer to various stakeholders, such as line managers, colleagues, suppliers, clients, and auditors. Each of these individuals or entities have their own expectations of quality when it comes to the delivery of products or services. However, no matter who the client may be, the intrapreneur is always determined to exceed these expectations and set a new standard of quality. This drive for excellence is what sets intrapreneurs apart from the rest. They possess a unique ability to identify opportunities for improvement and take initiative to implement new ideas and strategies that lead to better outcomes. Intrapreneurs are not afraid to challenge the status quo and push the boundaries in order to achieve the desired quality in their work. Moreover, intrapreneurs are not limited by their job title or role within the company. They are constantly seeking ways to add value and make a positive impact, even if it means going beyond their designated responsibilities. This dedication to their work and the company as a whole is what makes intrapreneurs invaluable assets to any organization. In conclusion, whether it is through their creativity, determination, or drive for excellence, intrapreneurs never fail to surpass the expected quality in their work. They are constantly striving to improve and exceed the expectations of their clients, ultimately contributing to the success and growth of their company.

Another crucial element of success in a career is the ability to effectively deal with other individuals. Whether it be colleagues, clients, or superiors, strong communication and interpersonal skills are essential for achieving one's professional goals. However, simply meeting the expected requirements and delivering satisfactory work is often not enough to excel in a competitive work environment. During a recent training session, I learned a valuable lesson about going above and beyond in our interactions with others. This concept, known as "<u>exchange in excess</u>", emphasizes the importance of exceeding expectations and providing more value than what is initially anticipated. By consistently delivering exceptional work and exceeding expectations, we not only build strong relationships and earn the respect of our peers, but we also set ourselves apart as top performers in our field. Furthermore, this practice of exchange in excess goes beyond the workplace. It extends to all aspects of our lives, from personal relationships to community involvement. By constantly striving to give more than what is expected, we not only benefit ourselves, but we also contribute to creating a more positive and fulfilling environment for those around us. In today's dynamic landscape and competitive world, it is no longer enough to simply meet expectations and get by. To truly succeed in a career, we must be willing to go above and beyond, constantly striving to deliver more than what is expected. By adopting the mindset of exchange in excess, we can unlock our full potential and achieve even greater levels of success and fulfilment in our professional and personal lives."

During the performance of a job, there is a fundamental understanding that certain tasks and responsibilities are expected to be fulfilled. These expectations can range from delivering goods within a promised timeframe, to preparing a comprehensive report that presents data in a specific manner, to meeting with a group of individuals to address a particular matter, to overseeing the manufacturing of goods, and even to keeping the office spaces clean and organized. As employees, we are accustomed to meeting these expectations and often base our actions and decisions on what is expected of us. In addition to these general expectations, there is also the formal agreement of a contract of employment that outlines the specific duties and obligations of an individual in their role. This contract is typically attached to a job description, which serves as a detailed outline of what is expected of an employee in their position. It lays out the key responsibilities, required skills and qualifications, and any other important information that is critical to the successful execution of the job. Ultimately, meeting expectations is crucial for both the individual employee and the company as a whole. It ensures that tasks are completed efficiently and effectively, goals are met, and the overall success of the organization is maintained. Without clear expectations and a solid understanding of what is required, it becomes challenging to produce the desired results and can lead to confusion and frustration for all parties involved. Therefore, it is important for both employees and employers to communicate and establish realistic and achievable expectations to ensure a smooth and productive work environment.

Upon deeper contemplation, it becomes increasingly clear that simply meeting expectations will ultimately result in maintaining the status quo for both ourselves and the company. It is the additional effort and dedication that propels us towards progress, isn't it? This is because business is fundamentally driven by people, for people, and between people. We all have certain expectations from others, and it is the fulfilment of those expectations that keeps things functioning smoothly. However, it is the willingness to go above and beyond that truly sets us apart and propels us towards growth and success.

The perception of a consistently over-delivering individual is immediately elevated and admired. Others may view them as dependable, hardworking, and dedicated individuals who always go above and beyond. This can lead to increased trust, admiration, and respect from colleagues and superiors alike. Furthermore, consistently exceeding expectations can also have a positive impact on one's personal brand and reputation. It shows a strong work ethic and a commitment to excellence, which can open up new opportunities and career advancements. Moreover, a person who consistently over-delivers can also inspire and motivate others to do the same. Their actions serve as a shining example of what is possible when one puts in the extra effort and goes the extra mile. A more productive and successful team or organization as a whole. On a deeper level, consistently over-delivering can also bring a sense of fulfilment and satisfaction to the individual. Knowing that they are consistently adding value and making a difference can bring a sense of purpose and meaning to their work. In contrast, consistently under-delivering can have a detrimental effect on one's reputation and relationships. It can lead to a lack of trust and respect from others and hinder career growth. In conclusion, consistently over-delivering can have a profound impact on how one is perceived and can bring personal and professional rewards. It is a trait that is highly valued and can set individuals apart in a competitive and ever-changing work environment.

Deliberately exceeding expectations allows one to maintain a dominant position and achieve a heightened sense of self-worth. This increase in confidence has a multiplying impact on abilities and admiration, paving the way for continued success. Going beyond the norm fosters a mindset of a lasting legacy, attracting others to seek out connections with you.

The intrapreneur consistently deliver exchange in excess. Gives more than take, delivers more than expected.

As the years pass and experiences shape our character, we come to embody the true essence of a good person. Our actions and decisions are guided by an unwavering moral compass, rooted in the fundamental values of honourability and integrity. These traits are not something we are born with, but rather something we cultivate and nurture over time. Through our interactions with others and the challenges we face, we continue to refine and strengthen our character, becoming shining examples of goodness and righteousness. Whether it be in our personal relationships or our professional endeavours, our unwavering commitment to honour and integrity serves as a beacon of light, inspiring those around us to follow in our footsteps. And as we continue on this journey of self-improvement and growth, we leave a legacy of goodness and virtue that will live on long after we are gone.

A foreign acquaintance, who happens to be a successful businessman, once shared with me his sense of pride in having maintained his original mobile number since its inception. This unique detail has become a personal advertisement of sorts, highlighting his consistency in fulfilling his obligations and settling his debts over the years. This has made him a rare asset in the country where he conducts his business. The mere fact that he has remained reachable on the same number for over three decades is a testament to his unwavering integrity.

The man's integrity is a rare gift in today's business world. With so many people prioritizing their own self interest, it is refreshing to find someone who remains true to his values and commitments. His integrity is a testament to his character and dedication to fulfilling his obligations and settling his debts. Over the years, he has proven himself to be a valuable asset to the country where he conducts his business. In a world where people are constantly changing and evolving, the fact that this man has remained reachable on the same number for over three decades is truly remarkable. It speaks to his consistency and reliability, qualities that are highly valued in both personal and professional relationships. His integrity has not only earned him respect and admiration, but has also made him a trusted and sought-after partner in business. Integrity is not something that can be bought or faked. It is a quality that is built over time through consistent actions and decisions. This man's unwavering integrity is a reflection of his strong moral compass and his commitment to doing the right thing, even when it is difficult. His reputation as a man of integrity has been earned through years of hard work and dedication, making him a valuable and respected member of the business community.

"In a world where trust is both more fragile and more valuable than ever, consistent and transparent actions build a currency of trust that is priceless." – Stephen Covey

Chapter 8

The Intrapreneur

An "intrapreneur" is an employee within a company who applies entrepreneurial skills and mindset to their role, driving innovation and growth from within the organization.

The term "intrapreneur" is a mix of "internal" and "entrepreneur," first coined by Gifford Pinchot III and Elizabeth S. Pinchot in a 1978 white paper.

Intrapreneurs use creativity, initiative, and risk-taking to develop new ideas, products, or services.

They operate within the framework of an existing company, leveraging the organization's resources and infrastructure, rather than starting a new venture from scratch.

Unlike entrepreneurs, intrapreneurs do not bear the full financial risks of their projects, as these are absorbed by the company. However, they still have the autonomy to work on innovative projects and may share in the rewards of their successes.

Intrapreneurs are responsible for generating new ideas, managing innovation projects, leading cross-functional teams, solving complex business problems, and assessing risks associated with their initiatives.

They must navigate the company environment, influence and collaborate with other employees, secure resources, and build alliances to execute their projects.

I hope this book has sparked your constructive thinking in becoming one of them, an "intrapreneur". Upon reflection on your soft traits and hard work, this content will help your progression at work but also in your personal life.

The personal growth of a colleagues is often closely correlated to the financial success of the business and this obviously depends by many factors, some of which you may consider beyond your reach. Remain "causative" and I trust your colleagues at every level of the organization will engage with 'the new you' and foster yours and the business' growth.

Below is summary handbook covering the main topics of each chapter, where you can scribble your notes on. Some recommendations follow for those more tactical daily activities.

I'd love to hear how these ideas resonate with your experiences. If you've had a moment of reflection, have questions, or need advice, feel free to reach out:

youtheintrapreneur@gmail.com

Handbook

The main topics of the chapters are summarised below. Please, use the empty space for your own notes!

Introduction

Small and medium enterprises employ a large part of the country workforce. This is why this book is likely for you!

Most SMEs are family owned and managed. The owners and directors of the company you work for, think very similarly to Andy.

Andy is relatable. A company owner and director with a varied experience and relative success, hands on and down to earth. He's your average business owner, director or employer!

Chapter 1

Intrapreneurial. An approach to your job that can transform your life.

Connect the dots. Think deeply about your knowledge and connections, connecting them delivers superpowers!

Sustainable. Deliver results without subtracting resources or opportunities from the future.

KISS. Keep it simple, stupid!

Chapter 2

Company. It has a much deeper meaning that 'legal entity' or even 'group of people who work together'.

Clear communication. Keep it clean, concise, simple and direct, avoiding everything that confuses the message you want to convey.

Verbal / written. The media you are using to deliver a message has an impact on how the message is laid out.

Talk to agree, email to circulate decision. Use meetings in person to discuss a matter and achieve an agreed decision. Circulate the decision over email. Don't discuss on emails.

Questions. An incredible tool at your disposal. Think how to engineer questions for the best outcome. They are crucial to understand matters better and to probe a topic or an opportunity..

Your character, your leadership. Enhance your person by building a character that leads to success.

Chapter 3

Strategy vs get s**t done. Long term plans are important, but stuff needs doing every day. Action, now!

Energy and action. High energy levels and dedication are crucial to keep delivering.

Problem solving and pushing hard. Setbacks are a way to learn from, push for a collective solution to learn and improve as a team.

Innovation and compounding. Small increments of improvements deliver big in the long term, thanks to their cumulative compounding.

Chapter 4

Data. In our era there's to much data available: navigate them carefully and focus on those few meaningful numbers. Don't loose your bearing.

Resources vs commercial success. Always keep commercial reasoning to decisions, deploy adequate resources.

Learn from fails, celebrate success. Every fail must become a lesson learned, every win and success deserves celebrating.

Detach and look at you. Watch yourself and your environment objectively, and spot improvements.

Loyalty. They key to long term success.

Chapter 5

Why. Find your why and share it with the business.

One. We are one person with one life.

Brain. It's your intellect that will deliver success to you and the business. Get tasks done and then always excel using your creativity, curiosity, intelligence.

Remote working. Interesting, but you may be worse off.

All agree. Beware of occasions when everybody agrees. Either the environment doesn't allow free talk or not enough thinking has gone into it.

Chapter 6

Hammer. Expand your toolbox, skillset.

Curiosity. They key to constant learning.

Lifelong learner. Life is a journey with a mix of daily tasks and new challenges. Constant learning enhance the human being.

Causativity. You own everything that happens to you. Control your destiny.

Appearance & social media. Let your appearance reflect your qualities and ambitions. Don't let yourself down.

Chapter 7

Exchange in excess. Deliver more than what is expected off you. Applies to family member, friends, colleagues, clients, suppliers...

Honour. Make certain that what you do makes others speak highly of you.

Integrity. The backbone of any successful person that leave others and the society better off.

Recommendations

Guidelines for working effectively with a typical owner-director.

Values: Uphold high standards grounded in integrity, ensuring your actions consistently align with your principles.

Safety: A strong commitment to safety forms the foundation of long-term success and fosters loyalty within your team.

Sustainability: Strive to deliver results while preserving relationships and resources, encouraging eco-friendly behaviours through your actions.

Dedication: Demonstrate a level of commitment and hard work that exceeds the expectations set by those leading the way.

Pride: The word often carries a selfish twist. Honor, however, acknowledges the contributions of others in our achievements.
For example, instead of saying, "I'm proud to announce our new product" go for "It's an honour to present what our team has created."

Stay ahead: Always stay one step ahead of me in thinking and identifying key business topics. This demonstrates that your intellect is driving innovation, and is not just focused on task execution.

Talk Causatively: Avoid saying, "You didn't understand me". Instead, say "I didn't explain myself well". This shifts the ownership of the situation and fosters better communication, constructive relationships.

Constructive: Always stay constructive. This can be especially tricky in challenging situations. Focus relentlessly on the search for solutions and new opportunities.

Manners: Politeness is essential. When speaking with me and for this matter, anyone, avoid distractions like your smartwatch vibrating or beeping —give your full attention.

Attire: Dress to represent the business and reflect your character, capabilities, responsibilities, and commitment to growth.

Time: Never be late. Plan to arrive early, then wait if necessary. "Traffic was bad" isn't an excuse. Even for an internal meeting in the next room, arrive early. Even more so for video meetings -staring at a screen for even just 30 seconds waiting for someone is really odd!

Writing: Have a clear goal (inform, ask for an opinion or a decision) and form an adequate message. Think of the receiver, not yourself. For most messages, less is more; crafting concise sentences that say it all takes effort. Proofread before hitting 'send.'

Emails: Use the subject line to reveal the content and what you are informing or asking about, and keep it short. Then, the first line should clearly state what you're informing or asking about. Use bullet points to expand on the topic with context, but keep it concise to respect the reader's time.

Avoid using capital letters, as it can come across as shouting.

Email Forward: Don't fall into the trap of forwarding emails without changes. If it's worth forwarding, it's worth improving. Every time you just forward, you are making a 'digital postman' of yourself - that's not paid well! Change the subject, add a first line with your thoughts, and then include the original message below for reference.

Email Attachments & Files: Attachments often have unclear or meaningless names, like "SMKT1234," which don't indicate their content. Name files with clarity—use a date format (yyyyMMdd) to keep them in order and add a few descriptive words that clearly explain the file's content and purpose. Avoid using ddMMyy, as it will mess up the files order in the folder.

Naming Your Files: Always give your files meaningful, concise names. Think of them as assets—clear, intelligent names help keep things organized. For work-in-progress files, avoid accidentally sending the final version with confidential information by clearly marking it with something like "DO NOT SUBMIT." Also, consider who the document is for. I often receive files from suppliers named after my company without their name on it, which makes sense for them but not for me, they only thought of themselves... and I'm the client! When creating a document for a client, start with your company name (for the client's understanding), followed by the client's name (for your reference), and then include the rest—short and to the point.

Folders: Just like keeping your physical desktop clean and organized, ensure your computer's file system is tidy. Each folder should have a meaningful name and contain only relevant files and subfolders. Think long-term—your folder system should remain consistent over time, making it easy to navigate. A disorganized system leads to inefficiency.

Excel: Take time to think about column names—they should be clear and meaningful. Create a coherent story with your data and highlight key inputs and results only. Avoid using decimal places when they are not meaningful; for example, if the values are in the thousands, you don't want to show two extra digits on every single figure for the sake of decimals... they are irrelevant for the message that needs passing across.

Socials: Curate your online presence by telling a story of the character you want to project forward, showcasing both successes and failures. Avoid posting non-constructive content and be cautious about being tagged. Never post images of minors—wait until they are eighteen and still ask for consent. Socials have been around for just over a decade, how would you feel if I could go to the internet and find all of your pictures from when you were born? It is worth underlining that as soon as an image is on the internet, it can be screenshot and saved somewhere else, who knows where. If you upload it, you may be able to delete it, but there could be copies somewhere that are out of your control.

Social Messages: Different media platforms call for different approaches. It's okay to be less formal—don't be afraid to include humour or light-heartedness in your posts. A joke or something funny helps engage your audience.

Life: Avoid gambling, betting, and drinking daily. On social occasions, never drink too much. I am vaping I need to quit!

Calls: Calls are far more powerful than digital communication. Remember this when engaging with family, friends, colleagues, clients, and suppliers. Beware of AI: you can receive calls that sound legit but aren't.

Video Calls: Video calls are less impactful than in-person meetings; always go for in-person if you can whether it is with colleagues clients or suppliers. They can be practical to cut on travel, but they are much less powerful.

Meeting Physically: In-person meetings allow you to fully access the power of human communication, blending verbal and non-verbal cues. Use icebreakers and common interests to build genuine connections.

Meeting Colleagues: The same principle applies when meeting colleagues—in-person interactions are key to fostering stronger, more authentic relationships.

Working from the Office: It helps building a company culture, align with company values, and stay connected to the pulse of daily affairs. Maximize networking opportunities at every level of the organization.

Travel for Business: Business travel requires organization—dress appropriately, be punctual, and manage your expenses. Make the most of your time away by scheduling additional meetings, staying curious, and leaving those you meet with a positive impression. Aim to intrigue others with your character and create lasting memories.

Dinner Out for Business: Business dinners are an opportunity to build rapport and make meaningful connections. Enjoy a relaxed atmosphere, but balance interesting conversation with professionalism. Get to know each other beyond work and make it a memorable experience, while always maintaining a level of professionalism.

As we reach the end of this journey, I want to leave you with a reminder of values that have stood the test of time and continue to inspire people in business and beyond. The core values displayed at the Rockefeller Center in Manhattan were written by John D. Rockefeller, Jr. (1874-1960), the founder of the Rockefeller Center. These principles reflect the dedication, integrity, and commitment to excellence that have shaped not only his legacy but also the foundations of countless successful ventures.

By embracing these timeless ideals, you can foster not only personal growth but also contribute to the growth and success of those around you. I share them with you now, not just as a closing note, but as a call to action: to bring these values into your own journey, wherever it may take you.

I BELIEVE IN THE SUPREME WORTH OF THE INDIVIDUAL, AND IN HIS RIGHT TO LIFE, LIBERTY AND THE PURSUIT OF HAPPINESS.

I believe
That every right implies a responsibility; every opportunity, an obligation; every possession, a duty.

I believe
That the law was made for man and not man for the law; that government is the servant of the people, and not their master.

I believe
In the dignity of labour, whether with head or hand; that the world owes no man a living, but that it owes every man an opportunity to make a living.

I believe
That thrift is essential to well-ordered living, and that economy is a prime requisite of a sound financial structure, whether in government, business, or personal affairs.

I believe
That truth and justice are fundamental to an enduring social order.

I believe
In the sacredness of a promise, that a man's word should be as good as his bond; that character—not wealth or power or position—is of supreme worth.

I believe
That the rendering of useful service is the common duty of mankind, and that only in the purifying fire of sacrifice is the dross of selfishness consumed and the greatness of the human soul set free.

I believe
In an all-wise and all-loving God, and that the individual's highest fulfilment, greatest happiness, and widest usefulness are to be found in living in harmony with His will.

I believe
That love is the greatest thing in the world; that it alone can overcome hate; that right can and will triumph over might.

JOHN D. ROCKEFELLER, JR.
1874-1960
FOUNDER OF ROCKEFELLER CENTER

youtheintrapreneur@gmail.com

www.ingramcontent.com/pod-product-compliance
Lightning Source LLC
Chambersburg PA
CBHW071032240526
45469CB00006BD/2190